WILDLIFE

of the

NORTH AMERICAN DESERTS

By

James W. Cornett

NATURE TRAILS PRESS
933 Calle Loro
Palm Springs, California 92262

To Jean
James W. C.

TO SAMANTHA

Contents

Preface   5

Introduction   9

    Climate   10
    Adaptations To The Desert Environment   11
    Desert Habitats   14

Arthropods   17

    Scorpions   19
    Solpugids   23
    Tarantulas   26
    Brown Recluse Spiders   29
    Black Widow   31
    Mantids   35
    Conenose Bugs   37
    Cicadas   41
    Antlions   43
    Painted Lady Butterfly   45
    Sphinx Moths   47
    Eleodes Beetles   49
    Ants   53
    Wasps and Bees   55
    Centipedes and Millipedes   59

Reptiles and Amphibians   63

    Toads   65
    Desert Tortoise   69
    Banded Geckos   73
    Zebra-Tailed and Earless Lizards   77
    Desert Iguana   79
    Horned Lizards   83
    Chuckwalla   85
    Spiny Lizards   89
    Side-Blotched Lizard   91
    Whiptails   93
    Gila Monster   95
    Common Kingsnake   99
    Whipsnakes   101
    Gopher Snake   105
    Western Coral Snake   107
    Rattlesnakes   109

Birds   113

    Vultures   115
    Red-Tailed Hawk   117
    Prairie Falcon   121
    Gambel's Quail   123
    Doves   127
    Roadrunner   131
    Owls   135
    Hummingbirds   139
    Ravens   143
    Thrashers   145
    Cactus Wren   149
    Phainopepla   151
    Loggerhead Shrike   153
    Black-Throated Sparrow   155
    House Finch   157

Mammals   159

    Bats   161
    Skunks   165
    Coyote   167
    Kit Fox and Gray Fox   169
    Bobcat   173
    Ground Squirrels   175
    Kangaroo Rats and Pocket Mice   179
    White-Footed Mice   183
    Woodrats   185
    Cottontails   189
    Jackrabbits   191
    Peccary   195
    Wild Burro   197
    Deer   199
    Bighorn Sheep   **203**

A Final Comment   207

Selected Bibliography   208

State and National Park Animal Checklist   209

Preface

This book is a greatly expanded edition of <u>Wildlife of The Southwest Deserts</u> first published in 1975. My purpose has not changed: to provide a concise introduction to the commonly encountered animals of the five North American deserts. This edition, however, has been updated and enlarged. Over twenty animals have been added and nearly every section has been rewritten. Indeed, persons familiar with the first edition may not recognize this book.

In general, three criteria were considered in selecting an animal species or group for inclusion in the text. Species with a broad distribution in the North American Desert were favored over those with a limited distribution. Commonly seen or well-known animals were more likely to be included in the text than those that are secretive and little known to the general public. Finally, a concerted effort was made to include venomous desert animals since there is so much curiousity surrounding their habits and the threat they pose to humans.

As the author, I am responsible for the accuracy of the statements made herein. However, many persons have generously given of their time to review portions of the text and have improved its accuracy as well as clarity. My appreciation is extended to the following individuals: Bertin Anderson, Colorado River Laboratory; Richard Arnold, University of California at Berkeley; James Bacon, Zoological Society of San Diego; John Bassett, University of Washington; James Bednarz, University of New Mexico; Kristin Berry, U. S. Bureau of Land Management; Laurie Binford; R. Terry Bowyer, Unity College; Richard Bradley, The University of Sydney; Bayard Brattstrom, California State University at Fullerton; Bryan Brown, National Park Service; Leland Brown, University of California at Riverside; William Brown, Skidmore College; William Caire, Central State University; Clinton Campbell, University of Idaho; Erick Campbell, Bureau of Land Management; Glenn Carman, University of California at Riverside; Steven Carothers, SWCA; Keith Christian, Flinders University; John Coleman, Virginia Polytechnic Institute; Marilyn Colyer, Mesa Verde National Park; Evelyn Conklin, Hi-Desert Nature Museum; William Cooper, Auburn University; Wayne Costa, Barstow Unified School District; Bruce Cushing, Michigan State University; Martin Daly, McMaster University; Charles Davis, New Mexico State University; Mark Dimmitt, Arizona-Sonora Desert Museum; James DeForge, Bighorn Research Institute; Julie Dreher, Saguaro National Monument; Robert Drewes, California Academy of Sciences; Alice Drogin, Arches National Park; Richard Dulaney, Arizona-Sonora Desert Museum; Isaac Eastvold, Sierra Club; W. H. Ewart,

University of California at Riverside; Gary Ferguson, Texas Christian University; Deborah Finch, Rocky Mountain Forest and Range Experiment Station; Patricia Flanagan, Joshua Tree National Monument; Neil Ford, University of Texas at Tyler; Stanley Fox, Oklahoma State University; Saul Frommer, University of California at Riverside; Lorrae Fuentes, Palm Springs Desert Museum; Jerome Gifford, Springdale; Richard Glinski, Arizona Game and Fish Department; Richard Goeden, University of California at Riverside; Steven Goldsmith, Austin College; Richard Golightly, Humboldt State University; James Gore, The University of Tulsa; Michael Greenfield, University of California at Los Angeles; James Griffing, U.S. Forest Service; Harvey Gunderson, University of Nebraska; Neil Hadley, Arizona State University; David Hafner, New Mexico Museum of Natural History; Michael Hamilton, James Reserve; Eric Hanson; Gary Harwell, Arizona-Sonora Desert Museum; John Hermanson, Emory University; Richard Hill, Michigan State University; Norm Hogg, Blue Heron Enterprises; Robert Huggins, Big Bend National Park; Leon Hunter, Barstow Unified School District; Gary Ivey, U.S. Fish and Wildlife Service; Mark Johnson, Mississippi State University; K. Bruce Jones, Bureau of Land Management; Mark Jorgensen, Anza-Borrego Desert State Park; William Karasov, University of Wisconsin; Bill Kraus, University of California at San Diego; Lawrence LaPre', Tierra Madre Consultants; Fred LaRue, Sacramento Zoo; Howard Lawler, Arizona-Sonora Desert Museum; E. F. Legner, University of California at Riverside; Herbert Levi, Harvard University; Richard Mac-Millen, University of California at Irvine; Tim Manolis, Animal Protection Institute; Carl Marti, Weber State College; Brian Maurer, University of Arizona; Wilbur Mayhew, University of California at Riverside; V. Rick McDaniel, Arkansas State University; Rick McIntyre, Death Valley National Monument; R. T. M'Closkey, University of Windsor; Sherman Minton, Indiana University School of Medicine; Joseph Mitchell, University of Richmond; Robert Moon, Joshua Tree National Monument; M. S. Mulla, University of California at Riverside; James Murphy, Dallas Zoo; Allan Muth, Boyd Deep Canyon Desert Research Center; Ken Nagy, University of California at Los Angeles; Michael O'Farrell, Las Vegas; J. R. Oldenettel, San Diego; Virgil Olson, Death Valley National Monument; Robert Ohmart, Arizona State University; Ted Papenfuss, University of California at Berkeley; E. Davis Parker, McNeese State University; Kenneth Petersen, Iowa State University; Eric Pianka, University of Texas at Austin; Keith Pike, Washington State University; Frank Porter, Utah State University; Steve Prchal, Arizona-Sonora Desert Museum; Mary Price, University of California at Riverside; Paul Remeika, Anza-Borrego Desert State Park; Louis Riehl,

University of California at Riverside; Walter Rogers, Zion National Park; Rodolfo Ruibal, University of California at Riverside; Richard Rust, University of Nevada at Reno; Raymond Ryckman, Loma Linda University; Jim St. Amant, California Department of Fish and Game; Robert Sanders, San Bernardino County Museum; Karen Sausman, The Living Desert; Charles Scott, Saguaro National Monument; Kim Scribner, Savannah River Ecology Laboratory; Vaughan Shoemaker, University of California at Riverside; Harry Shorey, University of California at Riverside; Christina Spolsky, Philadelphia Academy of Sciences; Herbert Stahnke, Arizona State University; Robert Stebbins, University of California at Berkeley; Vern Stern, University of California at Riverside; Samuel Sweet, University of California at Santa Barbara; William Tanner, Brigham Young University; Lloyd Tevis, Rancho Mirage; Bill Truesdell, Joshua Tree National Monument; Renn Tumlison, Oklahoma State University; Joan Tweit, Tucson Audubon Society; Dennis Vasquez, White Sands National Monument; Terry Vaughan, Northern Arizona University; Phil Wagner, Ducks Unlimited; Robert Wagner, University of California at Riverside; Terence Wahl, Bellingham; Steven Waldschmidt, University of Wisconsin; Doug Walker, College of The Desert; Michael Wargo, Coachella Valley Mosquito Abatement District; Richard Webster, San Diego; George and Jeanette Wheeler, Ocala; Wesley Weathers, University of California at Davis; Richard Zweifel, American Museum of Natural History. Special thanks are extended to David Mathews and Jim Toenjes of the Palm Springs Desert Museum who read the entire manuscript and made numerous helpful suggestions.

The photographs used to illustrate the text were provided by numerous individuals. My thanks are extended to all of them. Credit for their efforts appear with the photographs. Uncredited photographs were taken by the author.

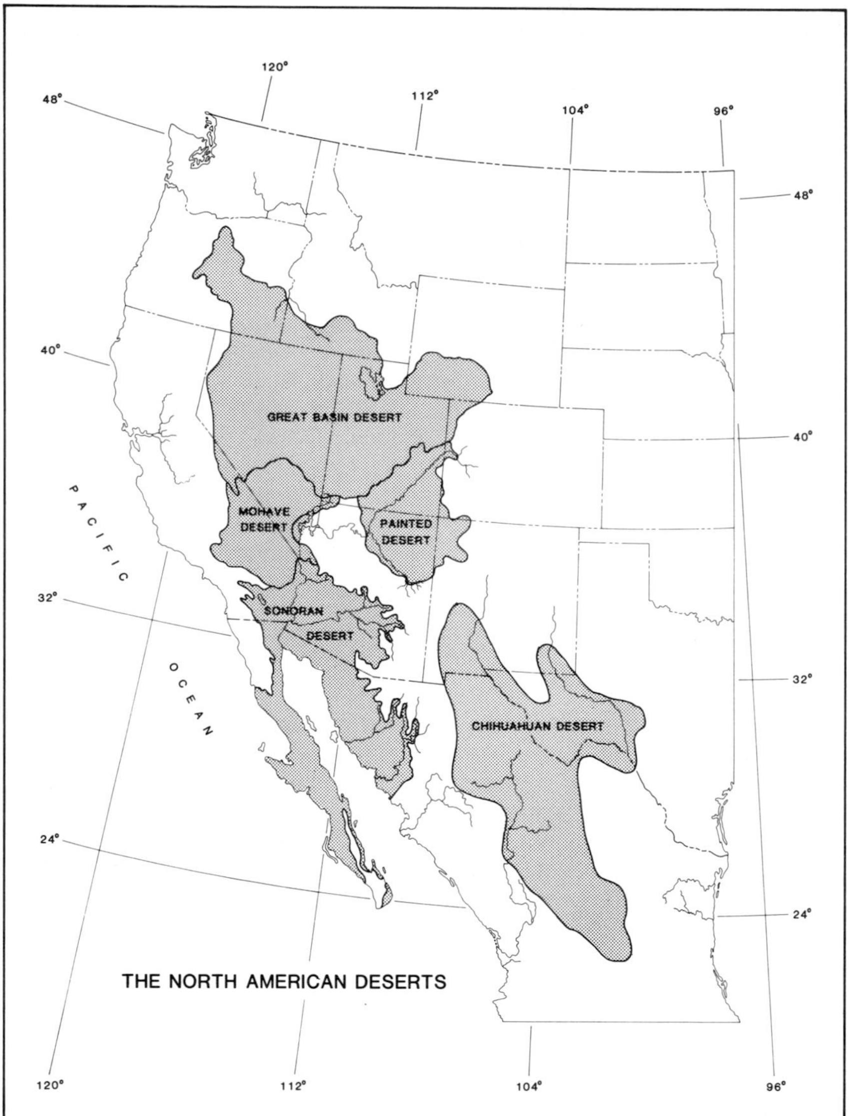
120°
48°
112°
104°
96°
48°
40°
GREAT BASIN DESERT
40°
PACIFIC
MOHAVE DESERT
PAINTED DESERT
32°
SONORAN DESERT
OCEAN
32°
CHIHUAHUAN DESERT
24°
24°
THE NORTH AMERICAN DESERTS
120°
112°
104°
96°

Introduction

The desert is one of the harshest environments on earth. Prolonged drought, exceedingly hot summers and radical temperature fluctuations are typical and would seem to preclude the existence of most living creatures. Yet the desert's variety and abundance of animal life is startling, especially to the uninitiated. Within Death Valley National Monument, which includes the dryest and hottest place in North America, there exist 4 species of amphibians, 36 reptile species, 140 species of birds and 57 species of mammals. Even more impressive is the fauna inhabiting the Sonoran Desert of southeastern California where rainfall totals just three to four inches a year and maximum temperatures average 110° F in July. Fifteen amphibian species are known to inhabit this region along with 52 reptile, 123 bird, and 68 mammal species. Both of these examples demonstrate surprisingly rich faunas and indicate that a wide variety of animals have succeeded in adapting to the harsh desert environment.

It is the purpose of this book to introduce the more widely-known animals of the North American deserts and to present their life cycles and the adaptive strategies they use to deal with the desert environment.

Climate

A desert is usually defined as a region which receives less than ten inches of precipitation annually. Using this standard, a line can be drawn on a map encompassing most of the southwestern United States and northern Mexico, a region known as the North American Desert. Because of its vast expanse and diversity of environments, it has been divided into five subregions known as the Chihuahuan, Great Basin, Painted, Mojave and Sonoran Deserts. The accompanying table shows the meager precipitation these regions receive.

Not only is Precipitation scant, it can also be erratic. For example, in January of 1948, Phoenix, Arizona, received no rainfall. Yet in 1949, January was the wettest month of the year with 1.71 inches of precipitation, over twice the long-term average for that month!

In addition to aridity, true deserts have hot summers. High temperatures result in rapid evaporation and it is high evaporation rates in combination with dryness that create desert conditions. The accompanying table gives the average daily maximum temperature in the hottest month in each of the five North American deserts. It should be remembered that these records represent temperatures taken in the shade,

Climate of the North American Deserts

	RECORD HIGHEST TEMPERATURE, °F	RECORD LOWEST TEMPERATURE, °F	AVERAGE DAILY MAXIMUM TEMPERATURE IN JULY (the hottest month)	AVERAGE DAILY MINIMUM TEMPERATURE IN JANUARY (the coldest month)	AVERAGE ANNUAL PRECIPITATION (in inches)	ELEVATION (in feet)
SONORAN DESERT						
Anza-Borrego Desert State Park Borrego Springs, California	120	31	111	39	7.19	775
Saguaro National Monument Tucson Mt. District, Arizona	116	13	100	39	9.62	2,560
CHIHUAHUAN DESERT						
Carlsbad Caverns National Park Carlsbad, New Mexico	111	-18	96	29	10.66	3,232
Big Bend National Park Panther Junction, Texas	110	1	94	35	12.81	3,750
MOJAVE DESERT						
Joshua Tree National Monument Twentynine Palms, California	118	13	105	35	3.34	1,975
Death Valley National Monument Death Valley, California	134	15	116	39	1.76	-152
PAINTED DESERT						
Arches National Park Moab, Utah	111	-18	99	19	8.00	3,965
Petrified Forest National Park Arizona	104	-27	92	21	8.69	5,440
GREAT BASIN DESERT						
Winnemucca, Nevada	106	-34	91	16	8.47	4,301
Dinosaur National Monument Dinosaur, Colorado	106	-36	93	1	7.50	4,750

three feet off the ground. Most desert animals spend their active periods on the surface where on hot summer days temperatures reach 150° F and under certain conditions approach 200°!

Although extreme heat and aridity are the obvious conditions that confront desert animals, cold winter temperatures must also be dealt with and, at times, can be an even greater obstacle to survival. The climatic table also presents the mean daily minimum temperatures, the month in which they occur, and the lowest temperatures ever recorded. As can be seen, many localities within the North American Desert regularly experience subfreezing temperatures on winter nights. Whereas record high temperatures may not result in animal mortality, record low temperatures can be expected to. Biologist Raymond Cowles found that many desert reptiles are killed by unusually cold weather and the winter mortality of birds during cold snaps is a well-known phenomenon. This feature of deserts is often given little consideration by naturalists.

ADAPTATIONS TO THE DESERT ENVIRONMENT

Desert animals must have water. Indeed, some require as much if not more than their counterparts in humid environments. Therefore any strategy for surviving in a desert must first involve obtaining water. There are three ways of accomplishing this. (1) Gambel's Quail, Wild Burros and Bighorn Sheep regularly visit springs during the hot summer months and maintain "water balance" by drinking. (2) A second group of animals is able to derive all necessary water by eating moist food. All foods contain some free water that is not bound up chemically. Even dry seeds contain 5% water and when stored in a humid burrow may show a 25% increase in weight as they absorb moisture from the air. Coyotes, Kit Foxes, Bobcats and other carnivores eat animals whose weight is usually two-thirds water. So long as they can capture sufficient food they can satisfy their water requirements by eating the moist tissues of their prey.

(3) A third source of moisture is derived from the breakdown of food and is termed "metabolic" water. All animals obtain water from this process as shown in the following chemical equation.

FOOD+OXYGEN > CARBON DIOXIDE+ENERGY+WATER

Simply put, food is "digested" (oxidized) resulting in the release of energy and the production of two waste products: carbon dioxide (which is exhaled) and metabolic water.

Only one group of vertebrates is able to subsist entirely on metabolic water--the Heteromyid rodents, a family that includes kangaroo rats and pocket mice, by far the most a-bundant mammals in the North American deserts. (Some white-footed mice may also have this capacity). The success of Heteromyids is not a result of any unusual ability to man-ufacture metabolic water since all animals derive the same amount of water from the breakdown of a given quantity of food. Rather, it is that they are so tremendously successful at conserving the water which is produced. It is this ability, the conservation of water, to which we now turn.

Conserving Water

In order to understand how animals can conserve mois-ture, we must first know how they lose it. There are four principle ways in which water is lost. (1) Many animals have sweat glands in their skin which exude moisture to prevent overheating. (2) As animals breathe and/or pant, water is lost from the moist surfaces of their respiratory tract. (3) Animals use water to void metabolic waste products and excess salt, either in the form of a liquid or as a paste composed of uric acid. (4) Finally, some water is lost in the feces. The avenue through which most water is lost depends upon several factors including surrounding temperatures, diet, and degree of activity.

For all animals, the greatest **potential** source of water loss occurs during evaporative cooling. Wild Burros and hu-mans keep their bodies from overheating by sweating. Al-though no figures are available for Burros, a perspiration rate of over one quart per hour has been recorded for a man walking in full sun on a hot day.

Many other animals including Bighorn Sheep, cottontails, jackrabbits, Coyotes and foxes evaporate water from their skin but even under conditions of heat stress this is a minimal source of water loss for them as they have no true sweat glands. These latter animals rely upon panting to keep cool. Both panting and sweating are effective cooling tech-niques but give up much precious moisture in the process. There are other, more efficient ways to keep from over-heating.

An obvious adaptation for avoiding the desert's intense

heat and reduce the need to use evaporative cooling is to become active at night when temperatures are cooler and the air more humid. Though in nondesert environments Coyotes and Gopher Snakes may be active during daylight hours, during the desert summer they can take advantage of the favorable nighttime environment and become nocturnal.

Conditions are also more favorable underground where temperatures may be 50° cooler than on the surface and where relative humidity often reaches 100%. A surprising array of animals seek subterranean homes including amphibians, reptiles, most mammals, and even some birds such as the Burrowing Owl. For those animals which do not use burrows to escape intense solar radiation, such as jackrabbits and most birds, staying in the shade is an obvious and important technique for reducing "heat loads." Even desert lizards, renowned for their sun basking and apparent preference for high temperatures, must seek shade beneath a bush or rock to avoid overheating on a summer day. Although other strategies are used to reduce the need to evaporate water through sweating or panting, the behaviors mentioned above are the most important and are used by nearly all desert animals to a greater or lesser degree. Other techniques will be discussed under the particular species of animal that use them.

Although animals can avoid high temperatures, and thereby reduce or eliminate water loss through evaporative cooling, there is little they can do to keep from loosing some water via urination--they must void the waste products of their metabolism. Thus, in practice, urination accounts for the greatest loss of water in most animals and any savings in this process can be of tremendous benefit. Pocket mice, kangaroo rats, jackrabbits and a few other mammals have evolved physiological and morphological adaptations for conserving water in this way. These animals have highly efficient kidneys which are able to concentrate salts and nitrogenous wastes in the urine to a much greater degree than can the kidneys of other mammals including man. This allows them to use less water in voiding wastes. In a related vein, birds and reptiles may be considered "pre-adapted" to a desert existence since their metabolic waste products are excreted not as urea, as in mammals, but as uric acid. The adaptive advantage of excreting this latter substance is that it has a low solubility in water and is voided in crystalline form. This permits the withdrawal of most of the water from the urine and results in the excretion of a semi-solid paste with a low water content. Thus the excretion of uric acid by birds and reptiles conserves water that is lost to mammals because they excrete urea.

The amount of water lost by most animals in their feces is generally small (on the order of three to six percent of their total water loss). Though some conservation of water can be achieved, the ability to reabsorb water from the feces prior to defecation is apparently restricted to just a few animals. These instances will be discussed in the sections on individual species.

DESERT HABITATS

Although many animals including ground squirrels, Mourning Doves, and kingsnakes, are found in a wide variety of habitats, most species have a preferred habitat where they may readily secure the food, shelter, and, in some cases, the drinking water they require. For example, Chuckwallas are confined to areas where large boulders provide cover and Phainopeplas can usually be observed only in the vicinity of mistletoe, their favorite food. Finding a particular kind of animal is predicated upon discovering its preferred habitat.

Desert habitats possess two basic qualities--substrate and vegetation. The substrate may be composed of sand, gravel, or boulders and be incorporated into dunes, washes, or hillsides respectively. Perennial vegetation may consist of low shrubs, cacti forests, tree-lined washes or streams, or some combination of these. The substrate can provide only shelter whereas vegetation can provide both shelter and food.

The Creosote Scrub community covers the flatlands of the Sonoran, Mojave, and Chihuahuan Deserts and, as its name indicates, is distinguished by the abundance of the Creosote Bush. The Sagebrush Scrub community is the most widespread plant community in the Great Basin and Painted Deserts. Only the three southern deserts have a true arboreal component in their vegetation--the Joshua Tree in the Mojave, the Palo Verde and Saguaro of the Sonoran and the Acacias of the Chihuahuan Desert. All five of the North American deserts have the common substrate features--sand dunes, washes, alluvial plains and boulder-strewn hillsides.

Saguaro forest in Saguaro National Monument

Dune habitat in White Sands National Monument

Arthropods

This group contains most of the animal species existing in the deserts of North America. Scorpions, spiders, insects and centipedes are arthropods and are characterized by a segmented body, an "open" circulatory system in which the blood is not confined to vessels, and a hardened outer skeleton or "exoskeleton" that is periodically shed as the animal grows.

Arthropods have evolved several structures and abilities that facilitate their survival in a desert environment. (1) Their thick exoskeleton is covered with a waxlike lipid layer that retards water loss. (2) Many arthropods can also close down their breathing tubes or "spiracles," thus reducing the amount of dry air that comes in contact with their moist, respiring surfaces. (3) Their metabolic wastes are excreted as uric acid which requires less water to eliminate than does the urea produced by mammals. (4) And finally, it appears they can reabsorb water from wastes in the rectum.

Scorpion

On warm evenings scorpions can often be found in surprising abundance. To locate them, one needs an ultraviolet or "black" light since they blend in perfectly with the substrate when illuminated with an ordinary flashlight. Under a UV light they fluoresce with an eerie, pale green glow that makes them stand out from every other feature in their surroundings.

The effectiveness of locating scorpions using this technique was illustrated during a field trip some students and I took to the Sonoran Desert of southeastern California. It was a warm spring night and after walking a short distance, using flashlights to find our way, we huddled together in a large circle. Everyone then turned off their lights and two of the students turned on portable UV lights. Walking around the perimeter of our group they located 46 scorpions within ten feet of where we stood!

Such abundance no doubt frightens the novice when contemplating a first-time visit to the desert. The venomous nature of scorpions is well known and the belief that all are deadly is widespread. However, in the North American deserts just one of the twenty or so species is dangerous, Centruruoides sculpturatus, sometimes known as the Bark Scorpion. This species is small, about two inches in length, and often found beneath the loose bark of cottonwood trees. In Arizona, 64 people died from the stings of these scorpions between 1929 and 1948 and in Mexico, where Bark and other dangerous species are more common, approximately 100 people die every year.

It is the stinger-tipped tail that injects the venom. When threatened, or attacking large prey, it is flicked over the scorpion's back and into the victim. Muscles force the venom out of glands located in the bulbous segment just behind the stinger and through two tiny openings near the stinger tip. When subduing prey, the scorpion uses its pincers, serrated on the inside edges for a better grip, to hold the victim while the stinger is shoved into its body. It should be noted that the tail is actually an extension of the abdomen, evidenced by the position of the anus on one of the last tail segments.

Venom of the highly toxic species from Arizona affects the nervous system of humans and causes convulsions, paralysis of the respiratory muscles and ultimately heart failure in fatal cases. Immediate symptoms include a general feeling of numbness or drowsiness, itching sensation in the nose and mouth resulting in repeated sneezes, and excessive production of saliva.   Later affects may include a contraction of the lower jaw muscles making it difficult or impossible to open the mouth, difficulty in moving the arms and legs, and a rise in temperature to 104° F.   In the rare fatal cases, usually involving the very old or small children, death occurs within eight hours.

Unlike the solpugids to be discussed later, scorpions have an elaborate courtship which may last for hours.   The first contact is initiated by the male when he clasps the female's pincers in his own.   So interlocked, they twist and turn in circles, looking every bit like two dancers both struggling to lead.   At some point the male deposits a spermatophore on the ground and maneuvers the female so that her genital orifice is directly over it.   As she comes to rest, her body weight and suction bring the sperm mass inside her.

Development of the young within the female takes anywhere from a few months to over a year, depending upon the species involved.   The ten to fifty young are born alive and clamber upon their mother's back.   They remain there from three to thirty days, until their first molt.   During this period the mother does not feed the young and they exist on nourishment from their stored yolk.

Scorpions prey upon other animals including solpugids, spiders, tarantulas and insects.   Occasionally they may capture and consume small vertebrates such as Side-blotched Lizards or blind snakes.   They are also cannibalistic and do not hesitate in devouring their own kind.   Eating is a gruesome affair.   In addition to their two large pincers, scorpions have a smaller pair of pincer-like chelicerae which emerge from the vicinity of their "mouth."   When small prey is captured, these are used to tear tiny pieces from the victim and place them in the oral cavity.   When large prey is involved the digestive process of scorpions takes place pre-orally.   Digestive juices are extruded out of the mouth cavity onto the victim, the food is partially digested, and the scorpion sucks the fluid into its digestive tract.

Scorpions are well suited for desert life.   To be sure, their nocturnal and subterranean existence are the most important factors contributing to their success.   However, they possess additional adaptations which further assist in water conservation.   They can resist desiccation better than some other arthropods as a result of a wax layer in their outer integument.   All animals lose a great deal of moisture when they breathe.   Scorpions, however, have an extremely low metabolic rate and thus a dramatically reduced rate of breathing. This enables them to close their breathing pores, called spiracles, if they become too dehydrated. In contrast to insects, the main nitrogenous waste product for scorpions appears to be guanine rather than uric acid. As a compound, guanine contains more nitrogen than does uric acid, and requires less water to void. Finally, upper lethal temperatures for scorpions are several degrees above those of other desert arthropods as they have been known to survive at a temperature of 113° F for over one hour. Hidden in their burrow they can exist for months without food or water and in fact it is believed that most desert scorpions feed for only three to six months per year.

DESCRIPTION: The stinger-tipped abdomen and large pincers immediately distinguish this arthropod from all others.

DISTRIBUTION: Found throughout the deserts of North America, in most habitats.

Desert scrub habitat in Death Valley National Monument

Solpugid with Desert Night Lizard

These are ferocious-appearing creatures. Large size, huge four-part jaws and a covering of prickly hair create an alarming first impression. As a result, there are probably more questions about this arthropod than any other.

Although solpugids are often mistaken for spiders, biologists have placed them in a category all their own. Several features distinguish them from spiders including the lack of venom, huge pincerlike jaws, the use of six rather than eight legs for walking and the possession of an unusually long front pair of tactile appendages known as pedipalps. They also rely upon their fleet-footedness for capturing prey, instead of silken snares.

Small insects, spiders, scorpions and related arthropods are the usual prey of solpugids. However, I once had occasion to witness a large, three-inch individual nearly decapitate a night lizard it had captured. The lizard had been hunting termites among the fallen branches of a tamarisk tree when it encountered the solpugid. Using its keen sense of touch and perhaps vision as well, the solpugid lunged out with widespread jaws and secured a hold on the lizard's neck. The struggling victim was no match and within seconds the solpugid's rotating jaws had killed the lizard.

As with most of the desert's ground dwelling inhabitants, solpugids construct burrows to escape the intense daytime heat. Normally they are shallow, not more than three inches deep, and are dug under rocks or other surface objects. Investigations by biologists James Gore and Bruce Cushing have shown that in some species it is the males which actually dig burrows; the females apparently expropriate abandoned tunnels. Perhaps reflecting this effort, males usually return to their burrow on successive days whereas females almost never use the same shelter. It seems both sexes move on to new foraging areas as they exhaust the food resources in their immediate vicinity.

With the coming of warmer nighttime temperatures in early spring, solpugids arouse from hibernation and begin searching for mates. Just how an individual locates a mate is unknown, but presumably odor plays a role. Courtship is very brief and the male's behavior must be precise or he risks being devoured by the larger female. The male titilates the female with his pedipalps, an act that seems to mesmorize her and enables him to move close enough to turn her on her side. He massages her underside with his jaws and then uses them to open her genital orifice. At this juncture he exudes a mass of spermotozoa on the ground, picks it up in his mouth, and then shoves it into the female's vagina. This ends the sexual interlude and at that point he must make his escape to avoid being eaten by his mate.

After mating, the female develops a ravishing appetite that causes her to feed until she can hardly move. Her extra energy requirement is necessitated by the developing eggs within her. Three weeks after mating, the female digs a burrow in which she deposits the hundred or so tiny white spheres. When she is finished, she abandons the eggs, leaving the hatchlings to fend for themselves.

Solpugids are often mistakenly called "vinegarroons." The latter animals are not as common and widespread in the North American deserts and resemble scorpions in that they possess pincers. Solpugids are abundant and lack pincers.

DESCRIPTION: Long, uplifted front appendages (pedipalps), pale yellowish color, and four, pincerlike jaws that are nearly as long as the rest of the body, distinguish this arthropod from all others. The name "solpugid" is of Latin derivation and means sun fleeing, an appropriate designation for an animal that is nocturnal.

DISTRIBUTION: Solpugids have a worldwide distribution in arid and semiarid regions. All of the North American deserts possess several species with at least one found in every habitat.

The huge size and hairy body covering of the tarantula gives it a frightening appearance and promotes an undeserved reputation. Not infrequently I hear individuals describe the tarantula as dangerous or even deadly, yet such descriptions are totally unfounded.

There are actually twenty or so species of tarantula in the deserts of the U.S. and all are harmless. It is true their fangs are large, up to 1/4 inch in length, but they are reluctant to bite humans. Indeed most species must be continuously abused before defending themselves. I am not particularly fond of handling spiders, but have held many tarantulas and must confess their gentle behavior is surprising in light of their appearance. They can be picked up, allowed to walk over an arm or shoulder, and even petted.

The venom glands of our desert tarantulas are small and the venom is not potent. In fact there are no records of anyone in the U.S. ever having been hospitalized as a result of a bite. In the worst situation, it is little more than a pin prick with few if any complications. By comparison, bee stings are severe and are usually accompanied by localized pain, swelling and redness.

Worldwide there are some 600 species of tarantulas and they are by no means restricted to deserts. Jungles, mountains and grasslands throughout most of the tropical and temperate world have their share of species. The largest comes from South America and can have a body length of 3 1/2 inches and a leg span of 10 inches. Some of these species inflict a dangerous bite. By comparison, our desert tarantulas are pygmies with a body length rarely exceeding two inches and a leg span of just six inches.

Tarantula venom is used to subdue and digest prey though it is the latter function which is probably more important. Tarantula venom is so weak that researchers noticed grasshoppers continued to jump and behave normally even though envenomated. In other studies, mice showed no ill effects either and in one case a mouse had been struck several times. This contrasts markedly with scorpion victims which are immobilized almost immediately after being stung. Digestion, then, is probably the most important venom function, with fang penetration being as important as venom in killing prey.

Tarantulas, indeed all spiders, have evolved an unusual method of eating. After a victim has been subdued, digestive fluid is vomited onto its body. Within seconds the fluid starts dissolving the softer parts and this, in conjunction with the injected venom, forms a kind of broth which is sucked into the tarantula's stomach. The process is repeated many times until all that remains of the victim is a hollow shell. The tarantula's normal bill of fare consists of insects such as beetles and grasshoppers. Its large size enables it to occasionally attack much larger prey and there are records of tarantulas killing small rodents, lizards, a small rattlesnake and even other tarantulas!

Hunting is uncomplicated and involves no sophisticated webbing or jumping ability as is the case with many other spiders. Most captures result when the victim stumbles into the tarantula's burrow or walks dangerously close to the opening. A short rush by the tarantula usually suffices to bring the prey beneath its opened legs, pedipalps and fangs. Apparently tarantulas recognize prey by touch or scent as they are nearly blind.

It is the tarantula's burrow that enables it to survive in desert regions. The fangs and pedipalps are used to construct a vertical shaft up to twenty inches deep and sometimes modified to veer off laterally after a drop of four inches. The tunnels can be identified as tarantula lairs by webbing attached to the sides of the one-inch-diameter entrance. During the hot daylight hours the spider lies quietly at the bottom of the hole where temperatures are cool. At night it climbs to the top or emerges and stands close to the burrow opening waiting for passing insects. With the coming of winter, the tarantula plugs up the entrance and becomes dormant for several months.

Tarantulas have been known to survive without any food for a period of twenty-eight months and so have little trouble getting through winter. They are relatively less tolerant of water deprivation, surviving a maximum of seven months in captivity without drinking even though moist insects are regularly eaten.

Courtship is a fall event and it is at this time when humans are most likely to encounter a tarantula. An adult male spider is abroad day and night as he searches for a female. To prepare for mating, he constructs a sperm web on which he deposits a drop of milky-white seminal fluid. His pedipalps serve as reservoirs after their tips have been dipped into the fluid. Upon finding a female burrow he taps the ground with his leg to announce his arrival and lure her out of her burrow. He then approaches her from the front while she raises her body and displays her fangs. He clasps these lethal weapons with spurs on the inside of his front legs. This enables him to raise her up so that he can insert one or both of his pedipalps into her genital opening. After a few minutes, the spiders separate carefully, seemingly aware of the cannibalistic tendencies of their species. Each sex may mate several times in a season.

The female does not deposit her eggs until the following May or June. She lays from 500 to 1,000 eggs which are placed in a protective silken cocoon. The spiderlings hatch in about one month and stay close to their mother for several days before leaving her burrow.

Tarantulas are our longest lived terrestrial invertebrates and do not even reach sexual maturity until eight- or nine-years old. The smaller males rarely reach ten years of age and die after the fall in which they mate. Females survive through many seasons and have been known to reach thirty years of age!

DESCRIPTION: A large spider with a leg span of up to six inches and hairy body covering. Usually brown or black in coloration.

DISTRIBUTION: Found in most desert habitats throughout North America.

Tarantula

Brown Recluse Spider - U.S. Army Photograph

Other than Black Widows, these are the only spiders that can be considered dangerous in the North American deserts. They became widely known in 1955 when physicians in Missouri were confronted with several patients suffering from severe skin damage at the site of the bites, and the death of a small child. Since that time much work has been done on the toxic qualities of the venom and its effect on humans.

There are probably twenty species of brown spiders (Genus Loxosceles) in the North American deserts although it is the Brown Recluse Spider, Loxosceles reclusa, that has been implicated in most serious cases. Unlike the Black Widow whose venom is neurotoxic, pain-producing, and effects the entire body, the venom of this species is hemolytic and thus has a localized effect on tissue. Typically, a bite does not constitute an emergency and victims are often unaware that they have been bitten. Symptoms may not appear for several hours or even days. Local swelling as well as a blister at the site of the bite are the first symptoms. In most reported cases a black, ulcerous spot eventually develops from which comes extensive sloughing of the skin and the exposure of the underlying tissue. The lesions vary in size from a small spot to large patches up to six inches in diameter. In the case of a 56-year-old man from Alabama the lesion had grown to ten inches when the man died five weeks after being bitten.

At least nine deaths have been recorded in this country and five of these occurred in Texas where there have been sixty reported incidents in recent years. This is a very low mortality rate but is roughly equal to that of the Black Widow. Fatal cases result from internal hemorrhages and kidney blockage due to the accumulation of hemoglobin in the kidney tubules. However, in the vast majority of cases the signs remain local and the wound eventually heals, although this may take several months. There is just one record of a victim's wound not healing, necessitating a skin graft. Fortunately, an antitoxin has recently been developed.

Brown spiders are rarely seen due to their secretive habits, small size, and habit of hiding in inaccessible retreats such as rock crevices, burrows or beneath litter. All species are shy and retiring and attempt to escape when encountered. Bites generally occur when a spider is accidentally trapped in a shoe, glove or other article of clothing.

Males are apparently as toxic as females and are about the same size. Loxosceles possess six eyes arranged in three groups of two eyes each, a trait which deviates from other spider groups both in number and arrangement of eyes. Various shades of brown describes their body color and, on some species, a peculiar violin-shaped marking adorns the cephalothorax. This pattern is responsible for them being called "violin spiders" in many parts of the country.

Females lay up to 300 eggs in a cocoon and apparently defend the eggs and hatchlings if necessary. They reach maturity in one or two years and have a lifespan of about four or five. Brown spider webs are large, tangled affairs, with a seemingly haphazard arrangement of the strands.

DESCRIPTION: The violin-shaped marking on the cephlothorax (front segment) is the best way to identify brown spiders. Both sexes have a body length of slightly more than 0.4 inch with long legs and pale brown coloration.

DISTRIBUTION: Perhaps most frequently encountered around human habitation but Loxosceles unicolor may be found in many desert habitats. Distributed throughout the arid regions of North America with the exception of the northern Great Basin Desert.

Black Widow

That such a common spider possesses one of the most potent venoms in the world leaves most of us shuddering at the possibilities of an encounter. Yet one's chances of being struck by lightning are much greater than dying from the bite of a Black Widow. Odds are a person would never get bit in the first place. Black Widows are timid, retreating into some crevice or corner at the slightest sign of danger. They are sensitive to harsh treatment of their webs and know the difference between man and insect when either comes in contact with the silken threads. Their venom works well offensively in subduing struggling insects, but defensively it is used only as a last resort, when other escape manuevers fail. Black Widows seldom leave their web.

Newspaper accounts occasionally tell of persons being bitten. In the U. S., between 1926 and 1943, there were 1,300 reported bites and 55 fatalities--a mortality rate of four percent. Victims may suffer from breathing difficulties, vomiting and agonizing pain in the stomach, thighs and groin. Children and the elderly are more susceptible. A five--year-old child died within 24 hours after being bitten. Older persons may suffer additional complications due to weak hearts and decreased resistance. If death occurs, it is usually because the breathing muscles are paralyzed and the victim suffocates. However, each victim reacts in a different manner and there is great variability in the toxicity of these spiders. For example, researchers have found the venom of Latrodectus mactans (the common Black Widow of the southern deserts) to be ten times more potent in November than in April.

One incident involving a close friend and a Black Widow is a typical case in many ways. While looking under boards around an old mine, my friend placed his hand on top of a large female spider. The Black Widow inflicted two tiny, red wounds on his finger. Initially, he hardly realized he had been struck. Then twenty minutes later the pain became very intense and he vomited several times. He was taken to the hospital where he remained for three days until his recovery was complete. This was only the first of three bites this individual received in six years! Each time the symptoms were the same.

Black Widows prefer dark environments well protected from wind and rain. Outhouses were once common homes for the widows as these buildings had all the necessary requirements--darkness, protection from the elements, and lots of flies on which the spiders fed. There are many cases on record where unsuspecting persons were bitten while using infested facilities. Tender body parts would be pressed against the spider with a resultant bite.

The Black Widow gets her name from the attack on her mate immediately after mating. Whether she actually becomes a widow depends entirely upon the male. Her groom must leave her web as carefully as he came. Any misstep could cost him his life. When he first reaches her web, he gently tugs the threads. This is a special signal which lets the female know a suitor is coming aboard. Actual mating is brief, the male fertilizing the female by inserting the tip of of one of his pedipalps into her genital orofice. Often the tip breaks off inside the female, preventing either sex from mating again. Next follows the male's treacherous tightrope walk to safety. If he isn't too taken with the whole affair, he will make it off the web; a misstep alarms the female who, if hungry, hastily attacks.

After mating, the female deposits from 300 to 500 eggs wrapped in a silken cocoon. The cocoon forms a protective covering around the eggs, reducing predation upon the maturing young. The silk used in cocoon making is amazingly strong, having a tensile strength greater than steel. The youngsters emerge in about thirty days, striking out on their own immediately. They look nothing like their parents, often being brightly colored and marked. They are venomous, but because of their small size and even smaller fangs, are not dangerous. It is at this time when the spiders move about looking for a suitable home. They are so tiny they have little difficulty in squeezing under doorways or crawling through insect screens. In most instances Black Widows enter homes when they are small, maturing in about six months to large adults.

The Black Widow web appears to be a messy, cross-hatched structure that nevertheless is very good at snaring insects. Insects often litter the webbing, all of which are neatly bound up, waiting their turn to be drained of their body fluids. Even though the female spider possesses a highly neurotoxic venom, most effective in subduing prey, she prefers to tie up her victims before giving them the lethal dose. When a meal becomes tangled in the lines, she quickly throws loops of thread around and around the struggling victim. Tiny "combs" at the end of her fourth pair of legs facilitates this flinging of thread. The insect is soon helplessly tied up and ready to receive the fatal nip from the widow's fangs. (The venom not only immobilizes the victim but also begins to digest it.) She then backs off and waits for the venom to take effect. When movement has ceased, she returns to suck out the predigested contents of her victim.

The body moisture of the widow's prey provides sufficient water for her survival in the dryness of her desert home. When insects are hard to come by, she retires deep into a rodent burrow and fasts for up to 200 days if necessary. During this period, her deteriorating condition is indicated by her shrinking abdomen. She is still able to capture food should insects become more abundant. A summer cloudburst or the onset of spring usually brings relief.

Most forms of wildlife have predators and the Black Widow is no exception. Some desert Indian tribes poisoned the tips of the arrows by rubbing them in the mashed bodies of Black Widows they had collected. Today, widows must contend with a host of lizard species that would like nothing better than to add a relatively large, juicy spider to their menu. Most notable of the lizard predators are the large alligator lizards (Gerrhonotus spp.) which relish the widows and even consume their egg cases. There is some evidence to suggest that lizards may be immune to the venom's effects. The widow's eggs are attacked by a tiny fly, Pseudoqaurax signatus, which lays its own eggs on the widow's egg case. Upon hatching, the fly larvae begin devouring the spider's eggs. At least three tiny wasp species are also known to parasitize Black Widow egg cases in a similar manner.

It might seem Black Widows have few redeeming qualities. Yet it has been estimated that a female devours 2,000 pesky insects in her one-year lifespan--insects which might otherwise be bothering humans. In addition, the silk produced by female widows was used for gunsights during WWII.

DESCRIPTION: Coal black color interrupted by the orange-red hourglass mark on the underside of the abdomen immediately identify the female Black Widow. Large females may have a length of 1 1/2 inch. The male spider, which unlike the female is not dangerous, is just one-twelfth of an inch in length and colored light brown with white flecking. The sexes are so different it is difficult to believe they are the same species.

DISTRIBUTION: Found in most habitats throughout the North American deserts.

Mantid - photograph by Hans Baerwald, courtesy Palm Springs
Desert Museum

Mantids

Mantids are predators and it is their powerful front legs, armed with double rows of spines, that enable them to capture flies, bugs, moths and other insects. When the femur (third segment) and the tibia (fourth segment) are folded, the prey is firmly grasped between the facing spines and held there while it is torn apart with the mantid's strong mandibles. It is these folded legs which have given mantids the curious prayerlike stance and the nickname of "praying mantid."

The cockroach ancestors of today's mantids evolved some sixty million years ago in a world filled with a rapidly expanding population of flower-loving insects. Numerous predators, including mantids, were evolving and took advantage of this emerging food source. They have become remarkably successful, with 1,500 species worldwide, nineteen species in the U.S. and at least seven species in the North American deserts.

The success of mantids is in large part due to their concealing coloration. Desert species are tan or pale brown, colors that match the plant stems on which they rest. This feature, coupled with their slender body form and ability to remain motionless for hours at a time, enable them to blend in with their background, looking more like a plant part than an animal. Insects sometimes land or even crawl on mantids, realizing too late that they have encountered a predator. With a flash of the forelimbs, such careless insects become prey. The mantid's camouflage also helps them avoid detection by the birds and lizards which may prey upon them.

Should a mantid be detected, it does not necessarily become a victim. A large mantid (some reach five inches in length) can be a formidable adversary and has an intimidating posture consisting of raised forelimbs, side to side swaying, and production of a hissing sound made by rubbing the dorsal part of the abdomen against the hind wings. Lizards and members of the cat family are known to be discouraged by such a display. A small mantid is more agile and more likely to escape predation by flying away. Birds may be thwarted when the mantid suddenly outstretches its wings during takeoff, revealing bright markings that startle a bird and may give the mantid just enough time to escape.

Mantid breeding behavior can be a bizarre affair which often ends in the devouring of the male. Ten days after its final molt, the male becomes a mature, breeding adult. Finding a female mantid, and mating with her, occupies the rest of his life. A female is not hard to find since she emits a strong odor that can lure him for a distance of at least 300 feet. Unlike many other arthropods which have developed a courtship ritual, a male mantid must approach the larger female with great caution, lest she mistake him for prey. The compound eyes of the mantid are good at detecting movement, but they cannot readily distinguish inanimate objects from their surroundings. Thus, as long as he approaches slowly and freezes when she looks in his direction, he can get close enough to mate with her.

When he is only inches away, he flies onto her back and grasps her tightly with his forelimbs. With the tip of his abdomen he activily searches for her ovipositor so that he can separate the valves and inseminate her. She remains quite passive at this time, in fact she hardly seems to know he's there. Union may last for several hours. If the female is in need of nourishment she may quickly pounce upon him after mating. If she has recently eaten, he may be allowed to escape. Often times the male fails to subdue her when he rushes in and is captured instead. She immediately starts to devour him head first. However, even though decapitated, his pulsating body succeeds in mating with the female, the mating act carried forth by nerve ganglions located in his body. The advantage to the species from this curious behavior is that the female is inseminated even if the male blunders in his initial approach. In addition, she is presented with a large supply of nourishment as she begins to develop up to 400 eggs. This maximizes her reproductive capacity and assures the species the greatest chance of survival. The expendable male has performed his function and is then recycled for the benefit of the developing young.

The female lays her eggs in a kind of foam container. This is attached to the limb of a tree or shrub and hardens upon drying. The eggs overwinter in this protective case and hatch out the following spring. Mantids live for one year, the male dying a few days after mating and the female a few days after laying her eggs.

DESCRIPTION: Tan or brownish color (some introduced species are green), slender body, and elevated head and forelimbs immediately identify these insects.

DISTRIBUTION: Found throughout the North American deserts in most habitats.

Conenose Bugs

Some of the least known insects of the North American deserts are the conenose bugs. At just one-half inch in length and of drab coloration, they are likely to go unnoticed. Yet in Tropical America they are responsible for transmitting Chagas' disease to seven million persons annually.

Members of the genus Triatoma subsist on animal and human blood which they obtain by inserting the stylets of their proboscis into the victim's capillaries. They are sometimes termed "kissing bugs" because they may puncture the tender skin of the lips. More frequently they take their blood meal from some other part of the face, back or neck. The insects feed late at night when their victims are asleep. They have a quiet flight and land, feed for up to nine minutes, and fly off without the victim ever realizing what has happened.

The puncture goes unnoticed in 56% of the victims, although 5% of the people who are repeatedly bitten develop severe allergic reactions. Others, approximately 24%, display severe reactions resulting from the foreign proteins injected with the salivary fluid. These reactions may include itching of the palms and soles of feet and eventually the entire body, flushing of the skin followed by urticaria, local and generalized swelling, vomiting, chills, partial paralysis, severe abdominal cramps and even unconsciousness.

Conenose bugs can be carriers of Chagas' disease which is caused by microorganisms known as Trypanosoma cruzi. Trypanosomes are in the droppings of infected conenose bugs, and related species, and the bugs invariably defecate while taking a blood meal. Often times the victim scratches the puncture after the bug has left, inadvertantly infecting the wound with the trypanosomes. The victim's fingers may also transfer the trypanosomes to the mouth, nose, or the highly receptive conjunctiva of the eye. Symptoms of the disease appear ten or twelve days after a person is infected and include swelling of the eyelids and face, fever, and anemia. In the chronic form, infection may last many years and can end with the victim's death as a result of chronic myocarditis.

Woodrats are an important food source for conenose bugs. In the Sonoran and Chihuahuan Deserts the incidence of Chagas' disease in these rodents is high. Indeed, it is likely that woodrats are the most important reservoir for the trypanosomes which cause the disease. Woodrats can tolerate an enormous amount of feeding by conenose bugs as shown by an animal which was able to gain weight in captivity even though being fed upon by 1,789 bugs in thirteen days. Not surprisingly, conenose bugs are most frequently found in the stick-nests of these rodents.

In the United States the disease is not a problem. Although conenose bugs are common, even in areas where the disease is widespread, only 45% of them are infected. In addition, the actual number of bugs that are likely to be found in close proximity to man is relatively small and the number that gain entrance to his dwellings is minuscule. Apparently only one case has been reported in this country and that occurred in Texas several years ago. It is likely that many more people living in or very near Mexico are infected, but, for whatever reasons, these cases go largely unreported. The number of infections increases dramatically as one moves south into Tropical America.

Conenose bugs are most likely to be observed in May when the winged adults are dispersing into new areas including homes near areas where woodrat nests are close by. This was the situation when I encountered my first conenose bugs. My family had moved into a home surrounded by long-established woodrat nests and found two of these bugs resting on our living room wall. The house lacked screens and the windows had been left open for several days before we arrived. Pet dogs and cats may also bring the bugs indoors. Entomologists have recorded fifty bugs from a single house in Utah, the high number no doubt partially accounted for by the man's two pet cats moving in and out of the house at frequent intervals.

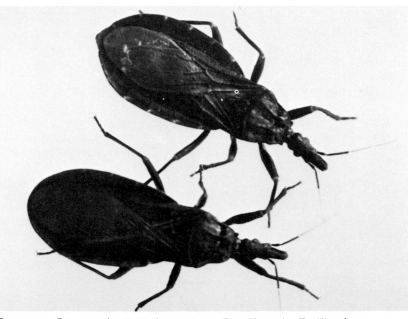

Conenose Bugs - photograph courtesy Dr. Sherwin F. Wood

Females lay from a few dozen to 600 eggs on the ground and incubation takes from 8 to 28 days depending upon the species and temperature. Newly hatched nymphs are wingless but develop these structures on their final molt, approximately one year after they hatch. When nighttime temperatures no longer exceed 60° F in the fall, the bugs become dormant and may overwinter either as eggs, nymphs or adults. They become active again in the spring and remain so until October. There is one generation per year.

DESCRIPTION: From one-half to one inch in length with protruding eyes and bodies that taper forward to a cone-shaped snout.

DISTRIBUTION: Found throughout the North American deserts in most habitats.

Apache Cicada

Cicadas

These insects are best known for the noise they emit during the hot days of late spring and summer. Some species produce an incessant buzzing, that is not likely to be confused with any other animal (although occasionally newcomers to the desert mistake the buzzing for that of a rattlesnake). The noise can be so intolerable that on those rare occasions when a cicada has been calling at night near my campsite, I forget my usual fondness for wildlife and drive the beast out of the area.

Only the male cicada calls. Muscles at the base of its abdomen vibrate a thin membrane at a high frequency and the resultant waves resonate in adjacent air cavities. The call functions to attract female cicadas so that mating may take place. When attacked by a bird or predatory wasp, the cicada also uses a piercing distress call that may be effective in discouraging enemies.

A female cicada lays her eggs on a stem or branch. The eggs hatch shortly thereafter with the tiny nymphs falling to the ground. Even at this stage the young resemble the adults although they lack wings and possess modified front legs adapted for digging. They immediately burrow into the soil and remain there for the next two to nine years depending upon the species. During their final summer, they return to the surface, crawl up a stem, and molt to reveal a winged adult. Although some cicada populations from the eastern United States are "periodic" with adults from any given locality emerging from the soil every thirteen to seventeen years, at least a few individuals of each of the North American desert species emerge every year.

Adult cicadas roost in trees or shrubs, often too high to be observed. The task of spotting them is made all the more difficult because of their concealing coloration which enables them to blend into their surroundings. One's chances of seeing a cicada are best if an individual can be found calling from a low shrub. All that is needed is a little stealth and patience since the insect suddenly stops buzzing when approached. Cicadas usually face away from the center of the shrub. All species are bumbling fliers in close quarters and have difficulty escaping from the tangles of plants unless they face outward. Such a posture minimizes the aerial maneuvers necessary to escape enemies. When in the open, they are fast fliers and may journey hundreds of miles.

Although desert cicadas show no apparent physiological adaptation to their environment, they do practice several behavioral strategies to obtain and conserve water. Adults suck the juices of plant leaves and stems in exposed locations at night rather than during the day when they would be vulnerable to predators.   In addition, they feed in shaded retreats during daylight hours and may rest on the down side of stems to avoid direct sunlight.   Through the hot afternoons, they rest in the center of shrubs where the temperatures are the most tolerable and the humidity greatest.   Of course most of the cicada's life is spent underground in a larval stage feeding on moist plant roots.   They experience a true desert environment for only a few, short weeks at the end of their life.

Interestingly, some cicada species call primarily at midday and thus decrease the chance of predation.   Normally cicada calls attract insectivorous birds.   But by midday most birds have fed and are less inclined to hunt when confronted with scorching temperatures.

DESCRIPTION: May be various colors but the large wings, broad head, one- to two-inch length and loud calls should readily identify these insects.

DISTRIBUTION: Found throughout the North American deserts in most habitats.

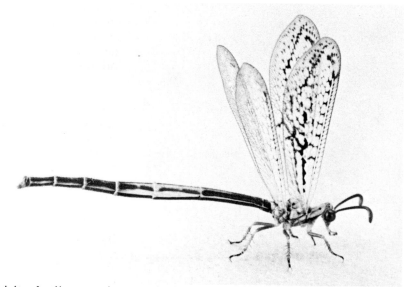

Adult Antlion - photograph by Hans Baerwald, courtesy Palm Springs Desert Museum

Picture yourself stumbling into a deep sand pit whose sides are so steep and unstable that you cannot stop your fall. As you slide to the bottom, a creature emerges from the earth and lunges at you with enormous sickle-shaped mandibles. You try to escape but an avalanche of sand takes you to the creature's open jaws faster than you can scramble up the walls.

Although this horrifying drama occurs every day, the creature is a half-inch antlion and, fortunately for us, the victims are not human. As its name indicates, ants are the dietary mainstay of the antlion. Workers stumble into the pits while foraging and are unable to escape because of the steep angle of the walls and the tendency of the sand to cascade to the bottom when disturbed. The antlion assists the avalanche by flicking sand on the slope above the wildly scrambling ant. Ultimately it winds up at the bottom of the pit, locked in the antlion's jaws. Struggle as it might, the victim cannot free itself even if somewhat larger than the enemy. The antlion's body is covered with stiff hairs that anchor it firmly in the sand, preventing the ant from pulling free.

The antlion is actually the larva of an adult form that looks almost nothing like the juvenile. Whereas the larva is stout, wingless and possesses huge jaws, the adult has small jaws, flies, and is long and delicate in appearance--in fact, it resembles a damselfly. (Larvae are sometimes referred to as doodlebugs because of the "doodles" or furrows they make in the sand as they walk backwards). The adults are most easily observed at night in the summer and fall congregating around lights.

An antlion larva constructs its pit in sand or silt, in a place free of obstacles that would impede digging. The tiny, inverted cone is created by the larva crawling backward in increasingly smaller concentric circles, occasionally using its jaws as a sling to toss out large particles. When it is finished, it buries itself in the bottom with only its mandibles protruding. Pits usually range from one to two inches in width and up to one inch deep.

In desert regions, the pits are usually located in the shade beneath a shrub. During the hot period of the day the antlion burrows deeper into the soil to escape the heat. At dusk they move to the surface, mend the walls, and eject any debris that the afternoon winds have blown into their pits. At this point they are ready to welcome their first victim. Not all antlions construct these traps; many species simply bury themselves in dirt or debris and snatch insects as they wander near.

The only enemy of the larval antlion of which I am aware is an insect known as the beefly. The adult lays its eggs near the antlion's pit and upon hatching, the larvae of the fly seek out the antlion and parasitize it, feeding upon the tissues of the host. Some species of antlions are found heavily infested with these insects.

Adult antlions do not feed, their only function being to reproduce and insure the survival of their species. Mating occurs in the summer or fall. Females lay their eggs on the ground and, in captivity at least, larvae may take up to two years to develop.

DESCRIPTION: The large, sickle-shaped jaws, backward walking and conical pit home immediately distinguish the 0.4-inch larva from any other insect. The adult has four wings that are held erect, a slender one- to two-inch body, and club-shaped antennae.

DISTRIBUTION: Antlions are found throughout the North American deserts, wherever there is loose, dry, and shaded soil.

Larva Antlion

Painted Lady Butterfly

The Painted Lady, <u>Vanessa cardui,</u> is one of our best known butterflies. Found throughout the North American deserts, indeed the world, its mass emigrations are legendary. In 1879, an enormous cloud of Painted Ladies flew from Africa to Europe with numbers so great it was said that their bodies darkened the sky. Spectacular swarms of this butterfly occasionally move through our deserts also. I once counted over three hundred pass through my field of vision in just sixty seconds. Millions of individuals are involved in these population explosions.

At least three such events have occurred in the North American deserts within memory: in 1958, 1968 and 1983. In each case emigrating hoards of Painted Ladies appeared after well spaced rains began in late fall. These rains resulted in the germinating of an abundant crop of spring wildflowers on which the butterflies fed.

During years of abundant food, butterflies living in northern Mexico and the extreme southwestern U.S. begin moving northward in midwinter. When a female's eggs have matured, she alights and allows a male to mate with her. She then lays her eggs--one to a leaf of appropriate food plants. Shortly thereafter both male and female die.

The eggs are remarkably resistant to desiccation and within a few days hatch and release tiny, greenish caterpillars with black spots and bristly hairs. They busily begin feeding on the host plant. Any one of several plant species suffices for the larvae of the Painted Lady, including lupines, mallows, Cryptanthas, and thistles. Young caterpillars protect themselves while feeding by tying the edges of leaves together with silk exuded from their mouthparts, forming miniature cups around themselves. Three successively larger homes may be built to accomodate them as they grow.

Within a few weeks each larva has reached its maximum size of one inch. At this point it affixes its hind end to the leaf of its last nest, hangs upside down, and changes into the next stage of its life cycle, the chrysalis. Within this protective case, each caterpillar undergoes a complete metamorphosis and transforms into a butterfly. By mid-spring the offspring of the immigrant parents crawls out of its chrysalis and begins the northward journey.

In good years the number of emerging butterflies swells as a result of the emigration of butterflies from the south, and a highly successful reproductive effort due to the abundance of food plants. Hoards of butterflies head north and, since they are fast flyers, travel hundreds of miles before expiring. Two main flyways exist. One heads up the eastern side of the Sierra Nevada Mountains into Oregon and Washington. The other goes up through Arizona and Utah and crosses the Rocky Mountains in southern Wyoming.

Although some Painted Lady populations are permanent residents in the desert, those that disperse generally fly north. Even in the Atacama Desert of Chile, located in the southern hemisphere, the ones which I have observed were always flying northward. Therefore it is incorrect to use the often heard term "migration" with respect to these insects since migratory animals return to the place of their departure. Painted Lady Butterflies "emigrate" from a region because individuals leave and never return.

Most generations of the original emigrants from the south move northward and there may be two generations per year. However, the number of butterflies dwindles as food resources return to normal and accidents and predators further decimate the emmigrant populations. Eventually those which reached the northernmost points are killed by cold temperatures and the populations once again reach equilibrium with the environment. Adults, pupae and eggs, overwinter in the southern deserts and adults can often be observed throughout the year.

DESCRIPTION: The adult's wings are stippled with orange, dark brown, and white and have a spread of slightly over 2 1/2 inches. Larvae are greenish-yellow with black spots and bristly yellow spines.

DISTRIBUTION: Found throughout the North American deserts in most habitats.

Painted Lady Butterfly

Sphinx moths are among the largest flying insects in our deserts. Adult wingspans can exceed five inches and the larvae may be just as long.

People are often intimidated by the striking appearance and actions of the larvae. Most possess a sharp spine on their hind end and a rather grotesque, fleshy body. All are stout and rear up their heads in a threatening sphinxlike posture if alarmed. When touched, they immediately turn and attempt to bite and if picked up exude a thick, green liquid from their mouth. Continued pestering causes them to curl up in a spiral much like millipedes. Larvae are, however, quite harmless.

Immature moths function as eating machines, hungrily consuming the leaves and stems of spring annuals. This fact was dramatically revealed to me late one afternoon as I drove out to a huge tract of dune primroses just east of Twentynine Palms, California. With no wind, it should have been quiet--as only the desert can be. But as I stood in the midst of the primroses I detected an odd noise that I had not heard before. I leaned over to examine one of the plants since the sound seemed to be coming from them. I immediately observed about a dozen sphinx moth larvae busily denuding the plant of its foliage and making surprisingly loud chewing noises as they did so. Other plants were also being devoured by the larvae. In fact, every single plant that I could see was being fed upon. In the still of that early spring afternoon the dominant sound was the chewing of thousands of sphinx moth larvae!

I returned to the spot two weeks later and found nearly every plant eaten to the ground for several miles in all directions. The few larvae that could still be seen were digging burrows in the sand. Within their burrows, they would pupate and in a few weeks emerge as adult moths. The size of the larvae population within a radius of five miles was estimated to be several million individuals.

Larvae change into adult moths underground and dig their way to the surface. Mating takes place shortly after emergence. The females lay up to 1,000 eggs on the underside of the leaves of food plants and within a few days the eggs hatch. In the southern deserts there may be time for two broods; one in the spring and a second in the summer. In the Great Basin and Painted Deserts only one brood is produced. Females and males die after they have completed their roles in the reproductive process.

The majority of sphinx moth species (Family Sphingidae) become active at dusk. At this time they emerge from their daytime hiding places and begin feeding on the nectar of flowers. Exceedingly strong and rapid wingbeats allow them to feed in a manner typical of hummingbirds for which they may be initially mistaken. (That these moths are strong fliers is attested by observations of them 500 miles out at sea!)

The sphinx moth's manner of flight, and the high energy required to maintain it, creates excessive heat in the moth's body, heat which must be dissapated. Most of the heat is lost through radiation and convection but about 10% is lost through evaporative cooling--by a moth regurgitating water droplets on its body. As has been discussed earlier, this is an expensive strategy in an environment where water is in short supply. However, adults feed exclusively on nectar and search out only those flowers which produce relatively large amounts of this excellent source of water.

Interestingly, in addition to utilizing flowers with a high moisture content, sphinx moths select species whose nectar has a sugar content of about 60%, nearly half again as much as that required by butterflies and almost twice that preferred by bees. No doubt this reflects the high energy requirements of a hovering style of flight.

DESCRIPTION: Hovering flight, heavy body, five-inch wingspan and thickened antennae identify these moths. Larvae have a prominent horn on their hind end.

DISTRIBUTION: Representitives of the family are found throughout the North American deserts, in most habitats.

White-lined Sphinx Moth

Eleodes Beetles

These beetles are some of our most conspicuous desert insects. Their 1 1/2-inch size, jet black color, and habit of wandering about in the open make them easy to spot. They are known by several names including stink beetle, circus beetle, and pinacate beetle. Stink beetle is derived from their ability to spray a noxious repellent from the tip of their abdomen. The substance consists of quinones and has a smell of kerosene. Ants, scorpions, and tarantulas are quite intimidated by the odor as they may initially rush the beetle but suddenly turn away at contact. (Apparently the beetle has a residue on its surface so that a full discharge is not always necessary. This is an important consideration in a desert since use of the defensive secretions can account for half of a beetle's daily water loss.)

If threatened, the beetle stands on its head and shoves its abdomen (hind end) towards the predator. This head-standing habit is the origin of the names circus and pinacate beetle, the second name meaning pinacle in Spanish. The only two regular predators of which I am aware are the grasshopper mouse and Black Widow. Not infrequently Eleodes becomes tangled in the widow's web at the entrance to a rodent burrow. The widow stays far enough away so that she can't be sprayed. When the beetle becomes exhausted, she ties it up by throwing silken strands around it. Even if it gets through her web and continues down the burrow she may sneak down later, after temperatures drop below 50° F. At this low temperature, Eleodes enters torpor and has difficulty escaping the spider. The grasshopper mouse, being much larger than Eleodes, rushes right in for the kill. It grabs the beetle along either side of its body and stuffs the abdomen into the sand. With the beetle's defense buried, it becomes easy prey for the mouse which proceeds to bite the head off and feed on the juicy interior of the beetle.

Eleodes beetles belong to the insect family Tenebrionidae whose members are commonly referred to as Darkling Beetles. This is a remarkably successful family, found throughout many of the world's deserts. "Darkling" alludes to the nocturnal habits of many of these beetles; however, most, if not all of our species seem to prefer daytime activity. In fact, it is only during the summer months, when daytime temperatures rise above 85° F, that they are abroad in the early evening hours.

Research involving desert-dwelling Eleodes have shown some interesting structural and behavioral adaptations. There is a space between the elytra (outer wingcovers) and the insect's body. This space seems to retard the transfer of heat from the environment since the temperature of the tiny air pocket may be 14° warmer than the interior of the beetle. No doubt this slows down the rate of heat gain and helps give it enough time to shuttle between shrubs on hot days without overheating. However, Eleodes' black color would seem to counteract any advantage accrued by the subelytral cavity. In full sun a black object absorbs 25% more heat than a white one. This certainly seems a disadvantage to an animal that maintains a body temperature below 90° F, much lower than air temperatures on a summer day. Eleodes maintains its body temperature below 90° F by staying out of the sun when temperatures are too high. It may construct a burrow for this purpose or amble down the burrow of another animal. Sometimes they clamber up the shaded stems of a bush where a breeze and the plant's own transpiration provide a cooler environment.

The black color helps in another way when the beetle stands on light colored sand. This is a form of advertisement that lets predators know that Eleodes is armed and not to be fooled with. The beetle's black color also helps during much of the year when the desert is cold and the beetle can benefit from being warmer. By tipping its abdomen toward the sun, radiant heat is absorbed, and at a rate faster than if it were white. This allows Eleodes to be active for longer periods--an important consideration during early spring when temperatures may be low but food availability high.

After their brief hibernation during November and December, Eleodes emerge from their burrow to search for food. They travel an average of about twenty feet per hour in this endeavor, with one beetle having gone 64 feet in a single hour. Eleodes is primarily a vegetarian, feeding on such plants as desert tea and buckwheat. However, they are certainly not adverse to consuming animal material. I have frequently seen them feeding on carcasses and once had the surprising experience of having them attempt to eat my hand! I had placed a pit trap in the ground as part of a research project involving desert lizards. Once each week I would check the trap to see what had fallen into the five-gallon container. One week a lizard had become trapped as had nearly 100 Eleodes beetles which, having nothing else on which to feed, devoured the lizard. When I placed my hand in to throw them out, they promptly bit me in mass, a sensation more startling than painful.

Females lay their whitish eggs in spring, depositing them in shallow holes in the soil and then covering them up. The glossy, tough-cuticled larvae or "grubs," remain in the soil feeding on plant roots. After an unknown period of time, they pupate and metamorphose into adult beetles and emerge from the soil in midsummer.

DESCRIPTION: Most species of Eleodes are about the size and shape of a slender black olive. The wingcovers or "elytra" on their back are fused making flight impossible.

DISTRIBUTION: Found throughout the North American deserts in most habitats.

Eleodes Beetle

Harvester Ant

Ants

About 10,000 species of ants exist in the world today. Of these, about 100 live in the North American desert region. Unlike some of their bee and wasp relatives, all ants are social creatures, living in colonies of from a few dozen to over a million individuals. The permanent members of the colony are females and are divided into castes, each caste being a slightly different size or shape such as workers, soldiers, and queens. Males are winged and are present in the colony for only a short time.

Probably the most conspicuous species of desert ants are the harvesters (genus <u>Veromessor</u>). These ants construct large craters around the opening of their nests, sometimes reaching diameters of two feet. Harvester ants feed mostly upon seeds although they must also capture insects to feed their larvae. The husks of the discarded seeds, along with excavated soil, are what form the craters.

Harvester ant queens prefer to dig their nests in exposed areas, such as along road shoulders or other barren sites which helps explain the ants' abundance in deserts. Tunnels may extend to surprising depths and there are records of them penetrating ten feet beneath the surface.

Ants are cold-blooded or "exothermic." They depend upon surrounding temperatures to increase their metabolism so that work can be performed. On cold winter days there may be no above-ground activity. When temperatures exceed 64° F on the surface some ants can be observed although they move slowly. On warm days their activity is dramatically stepped-up, reflecting their increased metabolism spurred by the hot sun and ground. Temperatures in excess of 111° F drive harvester ants underground. During the summer months harvester ants forage in the very early hours of the morning, retiring to their underground chambers by 8 a.m. In January they do not appear on the surface until 10 a.m. and forage only until about 2 p.m.

As mentioned previously, harvester ants feed on seeds which they gather in excess and store in underground chambers for later use. The North American deserts provide a bounty of seeds and there is seldom a shortage of this food supply. Biologist Lloyd Tevis noted that harvester ants living in his study area continued to find adequate supplies of seeds even though none of the kinds on which the ants were feeding had been produced in over a year! Workers from a single colony of ants may travel from 10 to 130 feet from their nest and collect 7,000 seeds per day. That works out to over 2,000,000 seeds per year.

Insects occasionally are eaten by harvesters, but because they cannot be stored as can seeds, their value is limited. Stray workers from different colonies fall into the latter category and may meet their demise if they wander into a neighboring harvester ant colony. Ants are territorial and defend their home ground against unwelcome intruders, especially workers from another colony of the same species.

Nearly everyone has been stung by an ant (though not all ants have stingers). Depending upon the species, a sting may have no effect on humans or a local reaction may develop usually accompanied with redness of the skin and itching. Deaths as a result of ant stings are exceedingly rare. Only four were recorded in the U.S. between the years 1950-1959. In all probability the victims were unusually sensitive to insect stings. Such persons usually die as a result of anaphylactic shock, an intense allergic response characterized by violent circulatory and respiratory spasms.

DESCRIPTION: Most harvester ant species in the genus Veromessor are shiny black in color. However, some species may be yellow, orange, brown, or red. Winged males and females on nuptial flights appear anytime from spring through fall.

DISTRIBUTION: Harvester ants, as well as many other kinds of ants, are found throughout the North American deserts in most habitats.

Wasps, bees and ants all belong to the insect order known as Hymenoptera. They are characterized by having two pairs of wings (although some females may be wingless), chewing mouthparts and, in females, an egg-laying structure, called an ovipositor, that has evolved into a stinger. As a group, they are important in the pollination of plants and many species of wasps are predators of noxious insects.

The largest wasps in our deserts belong to the genus _Pepsis_, some of which may reach 1· 1/2 inches in length. They are deep, metallic blue-black in color with bright orange wings. Because of their relentless search for large spiders, they are often called "tarantula hawks." Tarantulas provide food for the young wasps.

Female _Pepsis_ wasps can often be seen running on the ground checking the entrance of every burrow and rock crevice for a tarantula. It is thought that scent may play some role in helping her find a victim, but this has not yet been documented. If she is lucky, she may stumble upon a tarantula out in the open, but more likely she must find an occupied tarantula burrow. Aggressive wasps actually go down into the burrow to bring the spider out into the open.

Although a tarantula may be several times larger than the wasp, the wasp's quickness compensates for the size difference. As the battle begins, the tarantula seems dazed by the intensity of the female wasp's aggressiveness. Crawling all over the spider, she looks for an opening, a place where she can shove her stinger deep into the tarantula's tissue. In most encounters she is successful and the spider is left not dead, but paralyzed. The wasp then drags the tarantula to a previously constructed burrow. The limp spider is stuffed into the tunnel and one or more eggs laid upon it. The wasp's last act is to cover the entrance with dirt to protect her young. Within a few days the eggs hatch releasing tiny wormlike larvae which feed on the still living, though paralyzed, tarantula. When the larvae have reached the adult size they pupate and metamorphose into adult wasps.

It is interesting to note that tarantula hawks are species-specific. That is, each kind of _Pepsis_ wasp must find the right kind of tarantula. In captivity, an improper faceoff may result in the death of the wasp rather than the spider.

Another interesting wasp is the velvet ant, of the genus _Dasymutilla_. Not a true ant, it gets its name because of the female's lack of wings, antlike shape, and habit of

Pepsis Wasp - photograph by Hans Baerwald

Velvet Ant

running across the ground in broad daylight. She's covered with fuzzy hair which may be bright red, yellow, orange, black or white depending upon the species. The male has wings and is occasionally seen flying from one to three feet off the ground in search of a female. Both are active during the day and usually rest at night on trees or shrubs.

Females spend their adult life searching for the cocoons of other wasps or bees. When one is discovered, she lays an egg inside it. Within a short time the egg hatches and the velvet ant larva begins feeding on the host. The host wasp or bee, metamorphosing in its cocoon, is killed by this attack. When finally consumed, its space is filled by the velvet ant larva which will metamorphose in the cocoon.

Although they look adorable and may be tempting to pick up, don't! A hiking companion, unfamiliar with desert fauna, had accompanied me on an early spring outing in the Sonoran Desert. She had fallen behind and found a "cute" little fuzzy "ant" which she picked up. Her scream had me running back to her in time to see her gripping her wrist and the cute little "ant" scampering away. The initial pain was severe but subsided rapidly. She described it as like being hit on the hand with a rubber sole. A small red welt marked the spot on her finger where the wasp had stung her and the pain and tingling sensation were gone by the next day. Adult velvet ants feed on nectar. Captive individuals readily consume split grapes, honey and water.

Bee and wasp stings can be quite painful but are rarely serious. As in the case of ants, persons who die after having been attacked usually have been stung hundreds of times or are unusually allergic to the chemicals in the venom. Less than one person in a thousand falls into this latter category. From 1960 to 1969, 120 persons died as a result of bee and wasp stings in the United States.

DESCRIPTION: Wasps and bees can be recognized by their two pair of wings, chewing mouthparts and stingers. The order Hymenoptera contains the only stinging insects. (Scorpions are not insects though they do sting.)

DISTRIBUTION: Numerous species of wasps and bees are found throughout the North American deserts.

Centipede - photograph by Hans Baerwald, courtesy Palm Springs Desert Museum

"Here. Open your hand. I have something for you." O-bligingly, I held out my hand and inadvertantly allowed the young woman to drop a five-inch centipede into my palm. Within one second it was airborne as I jerked away in fear of being bitten. The woman was an enthusiastic student who thought she was holding a harmless millipede, not a venomous centipede. Fortunately, though it was in her hand for at least five minutes, she was not bitten.

There are around 3,000 kinds of centipedes with a species from tropical America reaching thirteen inches in length. No centipede from the North American deserts attains that length but the Giant Desert Centipede, <u>Scolopendra heros</u>, may reach nine inches--still large enough to make one pause at the prospects of being bitten.

The actual danger these arthropods pose to humans is often exaggerated. Laboratory mice die as a result of respiratory failure and paralysis when injected with the venom of some centipede species and the venom of many desert species is more toxic than that of rattlesnakes. But the fraction injected by even the largest centipede is incredibly small when compared to the amount of venom injected by most venomous snakes. Worldwide, there is only one authenticated death from a centipede bite. This involved a small, seven-year-old child from the Philippines who was bitten on the head and died 29 hours later. In the North American deserts, persons bitten usually describe the symptoms as intense local pain followed by swelling and redness around the bite and perhaps the bitten extremity as well. The intense pain diminishes rapidly with some residual sensitivity and numbness lasting up to three days. Bites do not usually warrant medical attention and are about as serious as a bee sting. It is widely believed that the sharp claw at the end of each leg is also capable of injecting venom but this is not true. Large centipedes may grasp with their legs resulting in tiny pinprick wounds but no venom is injected.

It is somewhat misleading to say that a centipede bites its victim. It actually pinches since it is the first pair of legs, not mouthparts, that is modified for injecting venom. Known as maxillipeds, they are powerful structures, heavily chitinized and much stouter than the other legs. They terminate in sickle-shaped claws. A cylindrical venom gland lies at each base and a canal leads from the gland to a tiny opening at the claw tip. When a centipede injects venom, it contracts abductor muscles that surround the glands and the clear, colorless venom is squeezed into the punctures.

The primary function of the venom is not defense, but to subdue prey. For the smaller centipede species, prey consists of insects and spiders. I have found large species which captured and devoured side-blotched lizards, geckos, small toads and even their own kind. They are also known to take young mice in captivity. Centipedes have poor eyesight (some are blind) and thus rely upon smell and touch to locate and identify prey. In one experiment, centipedes attacked small glass beads which were scented with fly odor but ignored the same beads which lacked the scent.

Hunting is done at night as centipedes are less tolerant of hot, dry conditions than are scorpions and some other arthropods. During daylight hours, in early spring and late fall, they lie hidden beneath surface objects such as rocks and boards. In summer they crawl down into deep, cool burrows. They are most active at night following summer rains and in captivity must be kept under conditions of high humidity and moderate temperatures or they die from dehydration. The sensitivity of centipedes to dry conditions is at least partly a result of their lack of an impermeable wax layer--a layer that is found in most other arthropods and functions to retard the loss of water. The lack of this covering may account for the relative scarcity of centipede species and numbers in the deserts of North America. Indeed, only a few large centipede species predominate as they have greater bulk and thus a more favorable water content relative to body surface area. This is helpful in buffering the effects of dehydration.

Centipede eggs are also quite vulnerable to dessication. If the relative humidity drops to only three percent, they perish. Perhaps to reduce this possiblity, the female Giant Desert Centipede constantly licks her clutch and stays wrapped around the forty or so eggs until they hatch. Her licking may also cleanse them of fungus which can destroy the developing embryos.

Mating probably occurs in spring. Contact and sexual recognition is accomplished with the antennae and is followed by the female leading the male around on a kind of courtship crawl. Eventually the male constructs a small web on which he deposits a sperm packet. The female then crawls over the packet and takes it into her genital opening. She deposits her eggs in a burrow and guards them for several weeks before and after they hatch. Curiously, if the female is disturbed while incubating, she devours the eggs.

DESCRIPTION: Although there are a number of important

differences, centipedes are often confused with millipedes. In the North American deserts, centipedes have a flat torso, one pair of legs per body segment, and are venomous. Millipedes have a cylindrical body and two pairs of legs per segment. Although most millipedes secrete a smelly repugnant fluid to repel enemies, they are herbivores and have no need of an offensive venom. Both centipedes and millipedes are commonly observed after rains. (Neither necessarily has one hundred or one thousand legs as their names suggest.)

DISTRIBUTION: Both centipedes and millipedes are found throughout the North American desert region, in most habitats.

Millipede - photograph by Hans Baerwald, courtesy Palm Springs Desert Museum

Painted Desert - Arches National Park

Reptiles and Amphibians

Moist skin without scales, two pair of limbs and aquatic larval stage characterize amphibians. Salamanders, newts, frogs, and toads are amphibians but only toads are widespread within the North American deserts.

Unlike amphibians, reptiles are completely adapted to a terrestrial existence. Their scaly body covering minimizes water loss through the skin and their shelled eggs allow them to reproduce on land. Tortoises, lizards and snakes are reptiles.

Reptiles and amphibians are exothermic or "cold-blooded" which means that their body temperatures, and thus their activity level, is dependent upon the temperature of their immediate surroundings. In most cases, this forces them to enter hibernation in winter and seek cover on hot days.

Red-spotted Toads in amplexus - photograph by Hans Baerwald, courtesy Palm Springs Desert Museum

Riparian habitat along the Rio Grande, Big Bend National Park

Toads require water in which to breed. Their larvae must grow and develop in ponds and the adults are most active after rains. Clearly deserts should be the last place to find toads. Yet these amphibians reach their greatest abundance and diversity in the North American deserts. No less than fifteen species are found in this region, more than in any other part of the U.S.; and at times they can be seen by the thousands.

One night in early September, I was driving towards Organ Pipe Cactus National Monument when I noticed increasing numbers of toads sitting on the road. With each passing mile more and more toads appeared until I could no longer miss them with my vehicle. Other cars had the same problem and the highway was littered with their carcasses. By the time I began braking for the monument turnoff the roads were so wet from their remains that my car went into a skid. Nearly every square foot of pavement was covered with living or dead toads resulting in hazardous driving conditions! I stopped the car and was awe-struck by the deafening calls of thousands of toads and the hopping about of hundreds more within the beams of my car's headlights.

The success of toads in the Sonoran and Chihuahuan Deserts is largely a result of predictable summer precipitation. When the rains arrive, there is a burst of insect activity--and toads eat insects. The toads emerge to take advantage of this sudden and temporary food resource and soon convert this energy into an enormous reproductive effort. Couch's Spadefoot Toads, Scaphiopus couchi, may capture enough insects in a single evening to tide them through the rest of the year.

Toads have only a few, temporary ponds which they can use for breeding. In the Southwest, such ponds are formed after summer rains, especially in roadside ditches that often extend for miles along highways. In such situations water is held for a few weeks, giving the toads just enough time to emerge from their underground retreats, locate an individual of the opposite sex, mate, and lay the eggs which insure a future population of toads. This frenzy of breeding activity frequently centers around roadside ponds, thus setting the stage for the carnage described previously.

A male toad's call attracts females to his location so that mating may take place. The two sexes meet in the water and the male grasps the female on top and from behind in an embrace known as "amplexus." During amplexus, she may exude over 1,000 eggs into the water as he simultaneously ejects sperm over them. Once the eggs are laid, the parents are out of the picture and the race is on--the eggs must hatch and the tadpoles metamorphose into air-breathing toads before the pond dries up. Fortunately, many desert toads have been able to evolve an egg that hatches rapidly, within twelve hours in the case of Couch's Spadefoot. The tadpoles of this species can transform into toads and hop out of their pond within ten days. (By comparison, a bullfrog tadpole takes two years to change into the adult form.) Much of the time the toads lose and the pond dries up stranding hundreds of tadpoles. But just as often the pond persists until each toad's metamorphosis is complete.

As a group, toads show great flexibility in initiating their breeding cycle. Red-spotted Toads, Bufo punctatus, breed from early spring through fall, whenever sufficient rain occurs to form ponds. Western Spadefoot Toads, Scaphiopus hammondii, in California breed in early spring following wet winters. In Arizona, New Mexico, and west Texas, toads breed through the summer wet season. (However, no toad species of which I am aware emerges on cold winter nights. Toads are not physiologically capable of breeding at air temperatures below 59° F and winter nights in the North American deserts are usually too cold.)

One reason a toad prefers moist surroundings is that it respires through its skin as well as through its lungs. By necessity, the skin is kept moist so that oxygen can move in and carbon dioxide move out. In dry surroundings, this results in a toad losing excessive amounts of water--up to fifteen times more water per hour than a rattlesnake and four times more than a kangaroo rat. If such a rate of water loss were to be permitted for even a few hours, the toad would die from dehydration. A toad minimizes such water loss by spending most of the year lying buried in the soil or hidden in deep rock crevices where cool, humid conditions prevail. In the case of Couch's Spadefoot, which lies buried deep beneath the sand near California's Algodones Dunes, two or more years may elapse before a summer storm finally brings it to the surface.

The problem of dehydration is partially ameliorated through the storage of water in the toad's bladder. At times, bladder water accounts for 30% of a toad's weight. Dormant toads can also store the waste product urea in their tissues rather than using water to expel it. The toad benefits from the stored urea since it raises the osmotic level of its body fluids above that of the soil moisture. This tends to draw water from the soil into the toad. Such an ability has perplexed scientists since urea can be toxic and would kill a human in the concentrations found in toads.

When toads awaken from dormancy and dig to the surface, they immediately rehydrate themselves, not by drinking, but by absorbing water through their skin. Most toads have a highly porous patch on their bellies which rapidly absorbs water. Within a few hours they are completely rehydrated.

Unlike frogs, toads appear vulnerable to predators with their chunky bodies and inability to leap more than a few inches. However, toads have a defense mechanism that involves wartlike glands that produce a toxic fluid. When disturbed a toad secretes this fluid over its body. Should a predator bite it, it gets a mouthful of poison--a poison that, in the case a giant Colorado River Toad (Bufo alvarius) can temporarily paralyze or perhaps kill a Coyote or Bobcat. (The Colorado River Toad can even shoot its poison a few feet by flipping its head downward.)

DESCRIPTION: Toads can be distinguished from frogs by their shorter legs, reduced webbing between the toes, and their relatively dry skin covered with glands or "warts." (These glands do not cause warts.)

DISTRIBUTION: As a group, toads are found throughout the North American deserts in most habitats.

Desert Tortoise, The Living Desert

Desert Tortoise

Tortoises are a remarkably widespread group with representatives on every continent and in most of the world's deserts. Their success is largely a result of their shells which enable them to move about and feed in situations where other animals would be vulnerable to predators.

This is not to say they are without enemies. Golden Eagles are known to take adult Desert Tortoises and ravens kill and devour juveniles. I occasionally find tortoise remains in Coyote droppings and have discovered tortoises with tooth marks on their shells. Individuals have been found with a limb or tail missing, probably the result of a Kit Fox or Coyote attack. But such attacks on adults must be rare and most likely occur when a predator is unusually hungry. A tortoise can withdraw its head and limbs almost completely within its shell and it might take hours for a canine to work one loose. Surely a predator normally finds a more rewarding meal with less effort.

As with most desert animals, tortoises deal with intense heat and aridity by avoiding extreme conditions and maximizing their opportunities to obtain moisture. In the spring they spend much time above ground feeding on the juicy green annuals which grow in response to winter rains. They may consume three to four percent of their weight each day as they rehydrate themselves by eating. Much of the excess moisture is stored in the tortoise's immense bladder. (A tortoise bladder can hold about one cup of water and it has been suggested that a man dying of thirst can obtain a life-saving drink from it. The bladder contents is also ejected into the face of enemies should the tortoise feel threatened.)

In early May, the desert vegetation begins to dry out but the tortoise continues to feed. By using the water stored in its bladder, it can continue to eliminate waste products resulting from food metabolism. Although humans and other mammals must suspend these wastes in water before voiding them, tortoises, indeed all reptiles and birds, can eliminate them as solids without suspending them in water. Tortoises can also withstand mild dehydration and tolerate a buildup of salts and other ions in their blood. Other herbivorous animals, such as Chuckwallas, soon die on a diet of dry food probably because they cannot withstand this kind of salt buildup and lack the water reserves of the tortoise. This tolerance to dehydration and capacity to store water help tide the tortoise through the late spring and early summer drought.

By June tortoises must begin reducing their food intake

and spend increasing amounts of time in their burrows. Cessation of feeding protects tortoises from accumulating toxic levels of waste products at a time when insufficient water is available to excrete them. By maximizing their time in their burrows they can dramatically reduce water loss from their skin and respiratory surfaces.

Just prior to a summer thundershower, a tortoise may emerge from its burrow and travel a short distance to a known depression where rainwater collects. (Some biologists believe tortoises deliberately enlarge the water holding capacity of these catchments by digging.) After the storm, the tortoise may drink until it has increased its weight by 43%. Much of the water is stored in its bladder.

As herbivores, tortoises eat most kinds of plants within their home range. However, they do have favorites. Legumes, including lupines and locoweeds, are frequenlty eaten and in the Mojave Desert plantago may comprise 37% of their diet. Grasses and the blossoms of desert composites, such as Desert Dandelion, are also frequently eaten and may be consumed when green and succulent or after they dry out in late spring. The droppings of jackrabbits, Coyotes and other mammals are also eaten on occasion. Young tortoises readily take insects in captivity, perhaps reflecting a need for foods high in protein.

Tortoises spend most of their life in their burrows which they construct by alternately scooping dirt from side to side with their front feet and kicking it out behind them. The diameter of the burrow opening usually reflects the size of the occupant and burrow lengths may reach thirty-one feet. In Utah, up to seventeen individuals have been known to use a single burrow. Most burrows are about ten feet long and house just one individual.

A tortoise does not breed until at least fifteen years old. Breeding activities commence in spring soon after the tortoise emerges from its four- to five-month hibernation. Rival males often engage in jousting matches at this time, using their gular horns to ram and push their opponent about, sometimes overturning them in the process. On smooth surfaces a victim may not be able to right itself and dies in the sun's heat. The largest and most aggressive male apparently does most of the mating, an act preceeded by a courtship which is not unlike male combat. The male approaches a female with his head extended and bobbed up and down. Zoologist Robert Stebbins relates that the male "nips at her nose, front feet, and edge of her shell and may lunge at her with his gular horn." The bottom of the male's shell is moderately concaved and this helps him mount the back of the female.

Most females lay their ping-pong ball sized eggs in May, June or July. (An adult female tortoise may lay a second clutch up to 1 1/2 years after mating.) From two to nine eggs make up a clutch. The eggs are deposited in a four-inch-deep hole dug at the entrance of, or within, a tortoise burrow. The hind feet are used to construct the hole. The female carefully covers the eggs with dirt and then urinates on the spot. This may mask any scent which would attract predators such as Gila Monsters, Kit Foxes, or Coyotes, all known to consume tortoise eggs. In approximately three months the eggs hatch and give forth offspring just 1 1/2 inches in length. Their shells remain leathery for the first five years at which time the young tortoises are quite vulnerable to predators. Only from two to five hatchlings ever survive to maturity.

Desert Tortoises remain in the same general area throughout their life. In Utah a tortoise has a home range of from 10 to 100 acres. In a study done in California, male tortoises were found to have home ranges of about 86 acres and females nearly 40 acres. Densities vary tremendously and it is believed that tortoises once numbered 2,000 individuals per square mile in the Mojave Desert. A more typical density would be from five to fifty individuals per square mile. The decline in tortoise numbers in recent years is largely a result of public collecting of tortoises and the destruction of both tortoises and their habitat as a result of widespread off-road-vehicle use on desert lands.

The lifespan of tortoises is not known though captive individuals have lived seventy years and it is likely they live much longer. The plate rings on their shells are not reliable indicators of age--some captive seven-year-old tortoises were found to have seven rings while others had eleven. Nor is shell size necessarily an indicator of age since the growth rate is dependent upon the quality and quantity of food and environmental temperature, factors which can vary from year to year.

As winter nears, tortoises are no longer able to maintain their body temperatures at the preferred level of from 80 to 90° F. Within two weeks of the first cold snap in October they return to hibernating dens or burrows and do not emerge until March.

DESCRIPTION: Stocky limbs, absence of webbing between the toenails, domed shell, and protruding plates beneath the neck (gular shields) distinguish the Desert Tortoise, Gopherus agassizii. Males are somewhat larger than females and weigh up to twenty pounds with a maximum shell length of about fourteen inches. (One huge specimen measured slightly over nineteen inches in length.) The much smaller Western Box Turtle, Terrapene ornata, is sometimes confused with the Desert Tortoise. However, the five-inch size and light and dark striping of the box turtle's shell are distinctive.

DISTRIBUTION: Found throughout the Mojave and Sonoran Deserts though conspicuously absent in some suitable habitat. Individuals have recently been discovered in the semidesert grassland in extreme southeastern Arizona. Requires at least a few patches of soil without rocks so that burrows can be dug. Gently rolling hills bisected by washes seem the preferred habitat. Not found above 4,000 feet. The Western Box Turtle is confined to the Chihuahuan Desert and the extreme eastern Sonoran Desert. This species reaches its greatest abundance on short-grass plains.

Western Box Turtle

Geckos are some of our most unusual reptiles. They emerge at night when most other lizards are inactive, emit pitiful squeaks if disturbed, and have translucent skin that give them a soft, fetal appearance. At first introduction, they seem ill-suited for life in a harsh, desert environment.

Yet geckos are abundant desert reptiles and found in a wide range of habitats from below sea level in Death Valley into Pinyon-juniper Woodlands above 4,000 feet. Because of their small size and nocturnal behavior, they generally go unnoticed. In fact, persons who have lived and camped in the desert for years and are familiar with most of the desert's animal inhabitants are often surprised to learn of the existence of these lizards.

The geckos' success lies in their ability to occupy a niche that no other desert reptile has exploited. Adjustments in behavior and physiology allow them to be active with body temperatures of about 84° F. This is nearly 18° cooler than the preferred body temperatures of most other diurnal lizards from the North American deserts. This enables geckos to forage for insects at night without competition from other lizard species. One drawback is that it does limit their range to the warm deserts (the Chihuahuan, Sonoran and Mojave) where evening temperatures stay well above 75° F over a large portion of the year.

In addition to insects, the gecko feeds upon spiders, newborn scorpions and other small arthropods. Prey is first stalked to within one inch, then captured in the jaws with a final lunge. While stalking, the gecko wags its tail in a curious felinelike manner. After a meal, it cleans its face with its tongue. A gecko also consumes its old skin as it peels off during the shedding process. Loose pieces are grasped in the jaws, pulled from the body, and swallowed.

The best way to see ground geckos is by slowly (and safely) driving paved roadways at night, especially during the spring months or following summer rains. They appear like tiny ghosts on the road as they seem to move in slow motion through the headlight beams. I have seen as many as thirty individuals in a single evening using this technique.

Like most of our desert lizards, geckos have a breakaway tail. However, they go one step further and wave it conspicuously about prior to an attack. This may be a very effective strategy when cornered by snakes which are often attracted by movement. In fact some herpetologists believe the leaf-nosed snakes (Phyllorhynchus spp.) capture more gecko tails than whole geckos. In such instances both reptiles come out on top. The gecko escapes and the snake gets the gecko's fat-storage organ; its tail.

There is a distinct advantage in the gecko storing so much fat in its tail. In the desert, food is seasonally available at best and quite unpredictable at worst. By hiding in the cool environment of a burrow, geckos maintain a reduced metabolism and may be able to survive for up to nine months on stored fat.

Male geckos appear to be territorial and in captivity fight continuously if kept in cramped quarters. During these encounters the aggressor squeaks as it attacks, apparently as an aid in driving away competitors. Voices are rare in lizards and that of the geckos may be associated with their nocturnal existence. The fact that geckos also have better-than-average hearing suggests that their voices are meant to be heard by other geckos, in addition to predators that can be startled by a squeal.

Breeding occurs in April and May, a few weeks after emergence from hibernation. It is not clear how males and females find each other but the laying down of scent trails by females is the most likely explanation. In mating, the male holds the female by the skin of her neck and curls his hindquarters under hers. Visible spurs near his cloacal opening may aid in sensing and maintaining the proper position for copulation. Two or three weeks after mating the female lays two eggs which she buries in the soil of a burrow. She may lay more than one clutch per year, perhaps three in favorable years. The eggs hatch in about 45 days.

DESCRIPTION: Although occasionally mistaken for young Gila Monsters, the tiny granular scales, dark bands or spots on a pinkish or pale yellow background, and vertical pupils distinguish ground geckos from all other lizards within the region. Adults measure from 2 1/2 to 3 1/2 inches excluding the tail.

DISTRIBUTION: Three kinds of ground geckos inhabit the North American deserts. The Big Bend Gecko, Coleonyx reticulatus, has the most limited distribution and is found only in Big Bend National Park in the U. S. The Texas Banded Gecko, C. brevis, ranges throughout the Chihuahuan Desert of New Mexico and Texas. Both of these species are associated with rock' outcrops. The Banded Gecko, C. variegatus, is the most widely distributed of the three and is found throughout the Mojave and Sonoran Deserts of California, Arizona, Nevada and Utah. It can be found in most desert habitats but reaches its greatest abundance along rock-strewn washes below 3,000 feet. (Recently, a new gecko has been discovered from the Sonoran Desert of southeastern California. Known as the barefoot gecko, Anzrbylus switaki, this species resembles banded geckos but is larger and possesses raised tubercles on its back. It is widespread in Baja California.)

Banded Gecko - photograph by Hans Baerwald, courtesy Palm Springs Desert Museum

Zebra-tailed Lizard

Greater Earless Lizard

This lizard is the desert's fastest reptile. Individuals have been clocked at speeds up to eighteen mph; outdistancing other well known speedsters such as Roadrunners and Common Whipsnakes, both predators of the Zebra-tail.

When traveling at top speed, a Zebra-tailed Lizard raises the forepart of its body completely off the ground and uses its back legs for running, a bipedal stance reminiscent of many dinosaurs. In this posture the front legs are held against the sides and occasionally touched to the ground to maintain balance. Not surprisingly, the hind legs are larger than those in front, with a more substantial musculature and unusually long toes to increase traction. The tail serves as a counterbalance, held high and curled over the back.

The alternating black-and-white bands on the tail, especially pronounced on the underside, account for the name Zebra-tailed. When pressed to the ground the tail, and indeed the entire lizard, blend beautifully with the sand and gravel on which it lives. Unless the lizard moves, it is nearly impossible to spot. Much of the time I nearly step on an individual before it reveals its location by sprinting away. However, with equal frequency the lizard raises its tail, curls it over its back, and wags it from side to side before taking off. I suspect it does this only when it senses that it has been seen or when it is too cold to run at top speed. The predator focuses on the conspicuously marked, but expendable and regenerative tail, and lunges for it. Although the predator may get the tail, the lizard escapes unharmed. Should the predator miss and pursue, it is likely to watch the easy-to-spot tail and thus fall for the Zebra-tail's next trick.

When chased, this lizard makes a sharp turn, and then suddenly stops behind a shrub. A predator only sees the tail disappear when the lizard turns, and is left confused as to the escape route taken. Unless the predator is lucky enough to stumble upon it again, the Zebra-tail's cryptic coloration is likely to hide it from view. Human pursuers, aware of this trick, will discover that Zebra-tails may eventually seek refuge in a burrow if pursued for five or ten minutes.

The concealing coloration of Zebra-tailed Lizards enables them to hunt in open areas with little risk of being spotted. They utilize a "sit and wait" hunting strategy. Typically, an individual rests on the substrate with forelegs extended so that it can see as broad an area as possible. When a beetle or grasshopper comes into view it rushes over and snaps it up. Interestingly, there is a shift in the kind of prey taken between Zebra-tails from the Great Basin Desert and those from the Sonoran Desert. Great Basin Zebra-tails feed primarily upon grasshoppers with beetles being the second most abundant prey. However, lizards from the Sonoran Desert feed primarily upon beetles with winged termites being the next most frequent prey item. The ability of this species to shift its reliance upon available food resources helps explain its abundance, second only to the Side-blotched Lizard, within its range. The niche of the Zebra-tailed Lizard is occupied by the closely related Greater Earless Lizard (Cophosaurus texanus) in the Chihuahuan Desert, and the Lesser Earless Lizard (Holbrookia maculata) in the Painted Desert.

The Zebra-tailed Lizard prefers a body temperature around 102° though individuals have been known to tolerate temperatures up to 115° F. In the morning, when still cold, a Zebra-tailed basks with its body held close to patches of warm earth. Later, when it has reached its preferred temperature, it stands with legs outstretched, allowing cool air to move between its body and the hot ground. Using these techniques on warm days, an individual lizard can keep its body temperature within a fairly narrow range.

Within a few weeks after emergence from hibernation, Zebra-tails begin their courtship activities. Males apparently attract females (and possibly ward off competing males) by showing off the bright blue-and-black-striped patches on their undersides. Copulation is brief, and results in females laying from two to six eggs a few weeks after mating.

DESCRIPTION: An adult Zebra-tailed Lizard may reach 3 1/2 inches, excluding the tail which is usually longer than the body. Flattened torso, long limbs, and black bands encircling the tail help distinguish this species. The Greater Earless Lizard reaches three inches in length, excluding the tail, and is distinguished by two black crescent markings on each side of its belly. The Lesser Earless Lizard is smaller, reaching just 2 1/2 inches, and lacks black bands on the underside of its tail. Both species of earless lizards lack ear openings.

DISTRIBUTION: The Zebra-tailed Lizard is common on open flats and washes of the Sonoran, Mojave and southern Great Basin Deserts. The Lesser Earless Lizard also prefers open habitats but is restricted to portions of the Painted, Chihuahuan, and extreme eastern Sonoran Deserts. The Greater Earless Lizard replaces the Zebra-tailed in the Chihuahuan and extreme eastern Sonoran Deserts.

The Desert Iguana, <u>Dipsosaurus dorsalis</u>, likes hot surroundings. This became dramatically clear to biologist Kenneth Norris while investigating the thermal tolerances of these reptiles. He discovered that Desert Iguanas commonly attain a body temperature of 108° F. and found one basking individual which had allowed its temperature to rise to 115° F., the hottest temperature ever voluntarily tolerated by a vertebrate animal. Such preferences for high temperatures probably explains their absence from the Painted and Great Basin Deserts which are high altitude, northern regions with long winters and only moderately hot days even in midsummer.

Not surprisingly, iguanas are the last lizards to emerge from their burrows in the morning. They are also the last to seek shade or underground retreats as the summer sun climbs overhead. Individuals spend about three hours per day abroad and spend the rest of their time in their burrow. I rarely encounter them in late afternoon, even in spring or summer.

Their need to maintain higher-than-average body temperatures is partially explained by their diet. Half their diet is composed of hard-to-digest plant material that takes much longer to break down into useable nutrients than does animal food. By maintaining the warmest possible body temperature for the longest period of time, these lizards maximize their ability to break down this material. They also eat their own fecal pellets, thus reworking predigested food and doubling the time it is worked upon by digestive enzymes. The ingestion of fecal pellets may also provide microbes for intestinal fermentation, a process that can result in the releasing of additional nutrients. Desert Iguanas have also been observed eating the droppings of woodrats, presumably for the same reason.

The assortment of plant material consumed by Desert Iguanas is quite large. In addition to Encelia and Creosote flowers, they eat the flowers, fruits and leaves of the Sand-verbena, Coldenia, and Sand-mat and the leaves of Dicoria, Indigo bush and Burro-bush. Individuals living near suburban areas don't hesitate in sneaking into backyards and eating Lantana (leaves), Oleander (flowers), and Pyracantha (leaves and fruit). Insects, including blister beetles and ants, are also important and in some regions make up almost half their diet. There are a few records of iguanas devouring smaller lizards and one record of a captive individual eating a new born rat.

Although they drink readily when water is available,

Desert Iguana - photograph by Hans Baerwald, courtesy Palm Springs Desert Museum

most iguanas do not have access to drinking water. Moisture is obtained from their food and through the metabolic process. While living in the Mojave Desert of California, our family "adopted" a large iguana that regularly entered our backyard to drink out of a pan we provided for wildlife. It came every morning and also became accustomed to our throwing out insects which it readily consumed.

Iguanas hibernate from late October until March, or about 42% of the calendar year. They survive by dramatically reducing their metabolic rate, beyond that expected for the temperatures they experience, and by utilizing their stored fat, which in most years is more than enough to get them through the hibernation period. Immature iguanas use shallower burrows than do the adults though all ages are surprisingly close to the surface. Most iguanas hibernate just four inches below ground level. This enables them to immediately sense the first warm days of spring and become active earlier in the year than if they were at greater depths. Of course this habit also subjects them to the effects of unusually cold winter nights and this may be lethal to small individuals.

Breeding activities commence in April. The territorial males aggressively pursue intruders and occasional battles ensue sometimes resulting in the loss of one of the combatant's tails. The loser is driven out of the area. Females are permitted within a male's domain and the dominant male may breed with more than one female. Females lay from three to nine eggs in burrows which they dig. After deposition the eggs are covered with soil and abandoned. Eggs hatch in about 45 days.

DESCRIPTION: This species is the second largest harmless lizard in the North American deserts with adults reaching a total length of 18 inches and a body length of up to 5 1/2 inches. From a distance they appear whitish but on closer inspection their upper surface can be seen to have gray or reddish brown spots or bars.

DISTRIBUTION: Inhabits both sandy and moderately rocky terrain but generally avoids steep hillsides. Distributed throughout most of the Mojave and Sonoran Deserts wherever its staple food, the Creosote Bush, is found.

Horned Lizard

These bizarre-looking reptiles are found throughout the North American deserts and, though often fairly common, they are rarely observed because of their concealing coloration and habit of lying motionless when approached.

Unlike every other lizard species of open, flat terrain, horned lizards do not have the ability to run fast. Instead, their survival strategy has been to hide from enemies by e- volving colors and patterns that enable them to "blend" into their surroundings. So important is this ability that they display a remarkable variation in color depending upon the substrate on which they live. I have found blackish indivi- duals in areas of extensive lava flows, reddish specimens from areas of red soil in the northwestern Mojave Desert, and orange-colored horned lizards from the Painted Desert. It's not surprising that these reptiles are frequently missed and only found when they scurry out from under one's feet.

Should their camouflage fail, horned lizards may still a- void predation because of the dozens of spikelike scales on their head. So effective is this armament that I don't know of any snake that can be said to regularly prey upon adult horned lizards. In captivity, lizard-eating snakes consistently refuse to devour horned lizards. I recall one instance where a kingsnake attempted to swallow one, but when it worked its upper jaw over the head spines it immediately released it, allowing the lizard to escape.

An even stranger defensive mechanism is used to deal with large predators. When handled roughly by humans, horn- ed lizards may expell blood out the corner of each eye. This is done with such force that tiny droplets of blood are ejected up to six feet, splattering the enemy. This has happened to me on two occasions and certainly was startling. Presumably, the behavior causes a predator to hesitate just long enough for the lizard to escape. There is some evi- dence indicating that the ejected blood may also contain a chemical that repells predators for the blood is known to cause pain and stomach cramps in canids and felines if swallowed.

Ants comprise the bulk of the diet of horned lizards and it is thought that such a diet has favored the evolution of a wide body form. Ants are considered a poor quality food and are constructed of much chitin which is difficult to digest. However, horned lizards have been able to utilize such a diet through the evolution of a stomach that com- prises 13% of their body weight, more than that of any other desert lizard. This enables them to consume and digest an unusually large quanity of ants so that they may meet their nutritional needs. Their resultant "tanklike" body form has in turn made running escapes difficult and has probably been important in the evolution of their concealing coloration and body armament.

Courtship and mating take place in the spring, following emergence from hibernation. All but one species, the Short-horned Lizard (Phrynosoma douglassi), lay from six to thirty eggs. The latter species gives birth to its young alive. Horned lizards are unusual in that females lay much larger clutches than do most other species of desert lizards. When young, their spines are not much of a deterrent and no doubt many are picked off by such predators as the Loggerhead Shrike, leopard lizard, rattlesnakes and whipsnakes. Perhaps the large clutches help compensate for the heavy predation of hatchlings. Young horned lizards emerge from their eggs in late July or August and usually reach sexual maturity within 22 months.

DESCRIPTION: A flat, stocky torso and numerous spines (especially on the head) distinguish horned lizards from all other reptiles.

DISTRIBUTION: Seven species of horned lizards occur in the North American deserts. Most habitats have at least one species.

Chuckwalla

Although awesome in appearance and size, these lizards are quite harmless. They are herbivorous, feeding on the flowers, fruits and leaves of a wide assortment of perennials including Creosote Bush, Burrobush, Dalea, Thornbush, and Encelia. In spring, Chuckwallas (Sauromalus obesus) forage more often upon annuals, taking advantage of the temporary abundance of these plants. Pincushion, Schismus Grass and Plantago are all annuals and eaten in spring if available. Flowers that are yellow in color seem especially relished.

The large size of the Chuckwalla is accounted for, in part, by its diet. It can extract only about 56% of the potential energy contained in a food mass --a limitation of its digestive system--and thus must have a relatively large torso so it can take in large amounts of leaves and flowers. By comparison, insect-eating reptiles such as Side-blotched Lizards and whiptails, can extract up to 90% of the energy from their food.

Life can be difficult for Chuckwallas when spring annuals are not available. In dry years little growth occurs resulting in meager forage with little moisture content. At such times Chuckwallas must get by on perennials alone. As even these dry out in late spring, the lizards become less active, in one study reducing the number of hours they were active each day from nine to five hours in the month of May. By late summer they may not emerge from their rock--crevice retreat for days at a time, keeping their body temperature down and reducing their energy requirements by as much as 70%--much as the Desert Tortoise does. This strategy enables them to survive on their stored fat reserves and conserve water until food becomes available again. In the case of Chuckwallas living in the Mojave Desert, this is not until the following spring. The seasonal activity period of these lizards can thus be short, from March through mid-August. Providing that July and August rains arrive, Chuckwallas living in the Sonoran Desert are active through the summer.

Chuckwallas obtain all their water in their food and do not even drink when water is available. As their food dries out in late spring, this poses a problem since they have little water with which to urinate out excess dietary salts. Both Chuckwallas and Desert Iguanas get around this by excreting salt into their nasal passages and discharging it out their nostrils. This gets rid of the excess salt and conserves water that can be used for other bodily processes.

The Chuckwalla is territorial. A dominant male, called a

tyrant, is the largest individual in a given area and behaves aggressively when an intruding male enters its territory. Usually some head bobbing on the part of the tyrant is sufficient threat to encourage another male to retreat. If the subordinate does not respond to head bobbing, he may be chased several dozen yards out of the area. Fights are rare, but when they occur, may last up to fifty minutes. Fierce biting can result in mortal wounds to the loser.

Successful defenses of territory· give an individual male the perogative to mate with all the females in his domain. The largest and most aggressive males are thus favored in that they produce a greater number of progeny than do other, smaller individuals. However, eventually even tyrants are displaced by younger, stronger males, perhaps their own offspring. Curiously, it seems that the size of the tail is of critical importance in determining rank. Tyrants that have lost a portion of their tail are soon displaced by nearby males. Biologist Kristin Berry observed this phenomenon among a population of Chuckwallas she was studying in the Mojave Desert:

"Male #36 was the dominant in a 50 meter wide by 5 meter high rockpile from 1968 through 1970. Although he was missing the left hand and forearm, #36 was a tyrant and courted the same female for three years. During the summer of 1971 his tail was chewed off, presumably by a predator. His tail length was reduced from 150 to a 53 millimeter stump. During 1971, #36 was inactive; he was observed basking and feeding but took no part in courtship, aggression, or head bob display activities. Another tyrant courted his female and pre-empted his rockpile."

Chuckwallas have few enemies other than man. Their strict association with rocky areas enables them to hide in deep cracks where they inflate themselves by gulping air. In such a condition they are impossible to remove from a crevice without ripping off one of their limbs. Their only common predator is the Red-tailed Hawk and only on Isla Angel de La Guardia, an island in the Gulf of California, do the hawks regularly make a meal of the twelve-inch Spiny-tailed Chuckwallas that live there. The Spiny-tailed Chuckwalla differs from the Chuckwalla of the mainland in being about 50% heavier and living in burrows in open, exposed areas. Their partially-eaten carcasses are not uncommon and no doubt the apparent heavy predation is a result of their relative vulnerability.

DESCRIPTION: With a body length up to eight inches, the

Chuckwalla is second only to the Gila Monster in size. Its flat body, brown, gray, and/or black coloration, and loose folds of skin on its neck and sides, distinguish it from all other desert lizards. Females and juveniles show faint banding, especially on their tails.

DISTRIBUTION: Found throughout the Mojave and Sonoran Deserts wherever large boulders occur at elevations below 4,000 feet.

Chuckwalla

Desert Spiny Lizard

At least seven kinds of spiny lizards (Genus <u>Sceloporus</u>) range into the North American deserts. As a group, they are found in a wide variety of habitats including sand dune margins, Sagebrush and Creosote flats, yucca and cactus forests, rocky canyons and Pinyon-juniper Woodlands. At least one of the seven species is found atop most desert mountain ranges. This broad tolerance of habitat types combined with a fondness for basking in open, sunlit areas place them among our most frequently seen reptiles.

All seven species are covered from head to tail with spine-tipped overlapping scales that can, at times, serve as protection from predators. There are actual accounts of snakes dying as a result of punctures to their throats while engulfing these lizards. However, the sharp scales are just as often not effective since I have also seen predaceous birds and mammals devour spiny lizards.

In addition to the sharp scales, a second defense mechanism has evolved among spiny lizards (and in a number of other lizard groups as well). It is a breakaway tail that wiggles violently after being pulled off. The predator can become so involved with the wiggling appendage that the lizard goes unnoticed and is able to escape. The tail breaks anywhere along a zone of weakness in several specialized tail vertebrae. Excessive bleeding is prevented by the constriction of the blood vessels after the tail has been pulled off. Eventually, it is regenerated. The success of a breakaway tail is evidenced by the large number of lizards seen with broken or regenerated tails. In fact, 30 or even 40% of the individuals in some regions have lost them and survive to grow a second or even third tail! Tail regeneration takes from two to eight months.

A male spiny lizard is distinguishable from a female by the presence of vivid blue markings on the male's throat and underside. These color patches are thought to aid in sex recognition: helping a female recognize a male and a male recognize another male. The color, or absence of it, is observed when an individual performs "push-ups," a bobbing movement caused by extending and then relaxing the fore-limbs.

An additional function of bobbing may explain its use at times other than during the breeding season. Unlike man and some other animals that possess binocular vision, the eyes of a spiny lizard lie on either side of its head. This eye arrangement makes it more difficult for the lizard to judge distances, since it has only one view of an object at any given time. (Humans have two views as each eye has a similar but slightly different perspective. This provides a three-dimensional quality to an object and thus gives a better idea of the spatial relationship between the object and its surroundings.) To compensate for this lack of binocular vision, the lizard bobs rapidly up and down so that more than one view is available at nearly the same moment. This helps the lizard judge distances more accurately.

Courtship and breeding commence in the spring and consequently most adult females are carrying eggs by the end of May. From five to fifteen eggs make up a clutch. Some high mountain species are live-bearing.

DESCRIPTION: Active, scaly lizards rather dark in color with short, wide heads. Commonly seen basking on rocks or trees. Adults are from 2 (<u>Sceloporus</u> <u>graciosus</u>) to 5 1/2 inches (<u>S. magister</u>) in length, excluding the tail.

DISTRIBUTION: Found throughout the North American deserts in most habitats.

Side-blotched Lizard

Side-Blotched Lizard

The Side-blotched Lizard, <u>Uta</u> <u>stansburiana</u>, is the only reptile likely to be abroad on calm, sunlit winter days. Its small size allows it to heat up rapidly and when cold it maintains a darker hue resulting in the absorbtion of additional solar radiation. As the morning progresses and the lizard reaches its preferred body temperature of 99° F, it becomes lighter in color which then helps reflect excess radiation and prevent overheating. Color change, altering posture in relation to the angle of the sun's rays, and movements in and out of shade help the Side-blotched Lizard maintain a fairly constant body temperature nearly identical to that of humans.

Once warm, Side-blotched Lizards can move about quickly enough to catch fast-moving insects such as grasshoppers, flies and moths. In addition to these insects they also consume large numbers of beetles, moth larvae and ants. Oddly, red harvester ants are usually avoided but large numbers of black ones are consumed. In one case an individual was observed to eat fifty in a two-hour period. Ants appear to be the staple food of juveniles. It is not known how they divide up this food resource with the much larger, and presumably more efficient, horned lizards that consume even greater number of ants.

Side-blotched Lizards feed whenever they are active, even in winter. Normally, they utilize the sit-and-wait strategy, much like Zebra-tailed Lizards. However, the latter species remain in the open and Side-blotched Lizards stay near rocks or shrubs. When prey appears they rush a few feet and snap it up. Occasionally, I have observed them jump in the air to capture a flying insect.

Many animals are considered "territorial" since they defend an area from intrusion by other members of their species. Side-blotched Lizards are no exception. Males establish relatively large territories during spring and attack and pursue other males who enter their domain. If one sits quietly watching them, it is not uncommon to see confrontations or even a pitched battle. The male whose territory is being violated first "displays" to the intruder but if this does not work an attack is likely. Over and over they roll, jaws clamped onto a leg or fold of skin. Within seconds the battle ends, usually with the trespasser being chased away and sometimes minus its tail. Occasionally, I have approached a Side-blotched Lizard, unaware that it was the subject of a display by a second, unseen individual. As the first lizard turned to run from me the second behaved as though it had frightened the first one, and chased and attacked the retreating individual. My presence had obviously affected the confrontation, perhaps changing its outcome.

Loosing its tail lowers an individual's social status much as it does the Chuckwalla's. But the loss of a tail may also save a lizard's life since a wiggling tail can provide a diversion to enemies. Side-blotched Lizards have numerous predators including the Roadrunner, Loggerhead Shrike, American Kestrel, Common Whipsnake, Common Kingsnake, and Glossy Snake to name only a few. The violently wiggling tail occupies these predators attention so that the lizard can escape down a rodent burrow or under a rock.

Side-blotched Lizards are the first reptiles to breed in spring and in fact are known to breed throughout the year in the southern deserts. Up to six clutches of eggs are laid and sperm may be stored in the female's oviduct for several months. This enables her to lay two fertile clutches without necessarily mating a second time should her mate be captured by a predator. Clutches consist of from two to six eggs. The high rate of reproduction is largely responsible for this species being our most abundant reptile. Side-blotched Lizards are short-lived; in some parts of their range individuals survive for only one year.

DESCRIPTION: These are small lizards rarely even six inches in total length. Males are various shades of brown and flecked with yellow and blue. In females the blue flecks are replaced with cream-colored stripes, chevrons or blotches. Most individuals have a large, dark blotch behind their front leg; hence the name Side-blotched Lizard.

DISTRIBUTION: Found throughout the North American deserts in most habitats. In the far west, these lizards seem to reach their greatest abundance in rocky areas. Individuals are often seen perched upon boulders for a better view of their surroundings and, in the case of males, to advertise their presence to other Side-blotched Lizards.

In contrast to the sit-wait-strategy for capturing prey used by most diurnal lizards, whiptails are active hunters. They are incessant in their search for insects: scampering from one shrub to another, digging beneath leaf litter, even climbing a short way up the branches of shrubs. They poke their snouts into every nook and cranny and incessantly flick out their tongues to smell prey they cannot see.

Because of their unique hunting method, the diet of whiptails is different from that of other insect-eating lizards. Large numbers of spiders and the larvae of moths, butterflies and beetles make up the majority of their food. Many of these are uncovered as the whiptail digs through litter or searches under objects. Adult beetles and termites are also eaten when discovered.

Like most lizards, whiptails have a breakaway tail that wiggles violently when pulled off. Interestingly, Western Whiptails (Cnemidophorus tigris) from the Sonoran Desert are more likely to use this defensive strategy to escape enemies than whiptails from the Great Basin Desert. This appears to reflect the greater variety of lizard-eating predators in the Sonoran Desert. For example, Gila Monsters, Glossy Snakes and Crissal Thrashers, all prey upon whiptails and are found in the Sonoran Desert. None of these lizard-eating predators occur in the Great Basin Desert. Lack of predators may also explain why Western Whiptails are more abundant in the Great Basin Desert than in the Sonoran Desert.

Another interesting difference between southern and northern populations of Western Whiptails involves the amount of time they are active each year. In the Sonoran Desert they are active through the summer. In the Great Basin Desert they become dormant during July and August. It is not clear why the northern whiptails become inactive. Perhaps the lack of summer rain results in too great a reduction in their preferred food. The Sonoran Desert receives much summer rain, has more plant growth and supports a greater number of insects through the summer months.

When pursued, whiptails move with surprising speed. Individuals have been clocked at fifteen mph for short distances. Typically, they run to the nearest bush when a human approaches. If the human happens to be a small boy intent upon catching his first reptile, the whiptail eventually seeks refuge in a burrow. Fortunately for whiptails, small boys seldom have the patience to wait at the burrow entrance to witness the lizard's emergence a few minutes later.

Whiptails dig their own burrows when they enter hibernation in late October or November. Depending upon the latitude and elevation, they push out the dirt plug and emerge from hibernation in March or April. Their preferred body temperature is 102° F and it is not until spring that solar radiation is sufficiently intense for them to reach this temperature on a daily basis.

Breeding commences in April and involves only those individuals that have reached two or three years of age. Females lay one clutch, of two to twelve eggs, per year. Of the eleven species known to occur in the. North American deserts, five are unisexual with no known males. These all--female populations do not need to mate since their eggs can begin dividing without penetration by sperm cells.

DESCRIPTION: Pointed snouts, extremely long tails, and a jerky gait distinguish whiptails from all other lizards within the desert regions of North America. Adults range from two to five inches in length excluding the tail.

DISTRIBUTION: Found in most habitats throughout the North American deserts.

Western Whiptail

The Gila Monster, <u>Heloderma</u> <u>suspectum</u>, and its close relative the Mexican Beaded Lizard of southern Sonora, are the only venomous lizards in the world. This fact, in conjunction with their large size and bizarre appearance, have given them a reputation for being quite dangerous.

Yet there are no reliable records of anyone ever dying from the bite of a Gila Monster. In fact few people have even been bitten by free-ranging animals. Most accounts involve persons who are handling captive animals thought to be tame. One of the most recent cases involved a twenty--year-old pre-veterinary student who was bitten on the hand by one of his five "pet" Gila Monsters. The reptile released its hold after fifteen seconds. Though the student washed the painful and profusely bleeding wound in tap water and attempted to squeeze venom from the bite, chills and nausea forced him to seek emergency treatment at a nearby hospital. One hour after admission, the victim's hand showed swelling to the wrist but this and the other symptoms were gone within 24 hours when he was discharged from the hospital. In other cases faintness, profuse sweating and vomiting have been reported.

As the largest lizard found within the boundaries of the U.S., the mechanical action of the bite alone can be quite painful. From 41 to 45 sharp teeth line the upper and lower jaws and with a viselike grip a Gila Monster is difficult to remove. Gila Monsters lack hollow fangs. However, their front teeth do have grooves which facilitate the movement of venom into the wound. In theory at least, the longer the lizard holds on, the more venom that is introduced.

Venom is produced by several glands in the Gila Monster's lower jaw. The toxin is partly composed of a chemical known as serotonin which, among other things, is a powerful pain-producing substance. Though the venom is quite potent, the lack of an efficient injection mechanism and the dilution of the venom with the lizard's saliva contribute to the successful recovery of victims.

This is not the case when small animals are involved. The venom causes massive hemorrhages of the eyes and kidneys and, to a lesser extent, the intestine and lungs. Severe heart and respiratory difficulties result and laboratory mice quickly succumb. Presumably the young of cottontail rabbits and roundtailed ground squirrels, typical small mammal prey, are also quickly subdued as a result of the venom.

The eggs of ground-nesting birds are an important food

of Gila Monsters. Stomach analysis has shown eggs to be the most frequent food item and numerous wild individuals have been seen in the act of devouring eggs of Gambel's Quail and Mourning Dove. Typically, Gila Monsters attempt to swallow eggs whole but usually end up breaking them and then lapping up the contents with their tongue. In the spring when eggs are readily available, adult lizards consume an average of one to two eggs per day and have been observed eating seven quail eggs from a single nest. It is interesting to note that Gila Monsters do not usually consume all the eggs in a nest if there are more than two eggs present. Rather, they forage at several nests even if they could have eaten the same number of eggs at a single nest. The adaptive value of this foraging method is unknown. In those areas where bird eggs are not readily available, Gila Monsters feed more often upon young rabbits and ground squirrels. Tortoise eggs are also eaten and there have been actual observations of tortoises defending their eggs from hungry Gila Monsters.

Most food resources preferred by Gila Monsters become scarce as summer nears, especially during unusually dry years. This was no doubt the stimulus for the evolution of their capacity to store enormous quantities of fat in their tail. Like the Desert Tortoise and Chuckwalla, Gila Monsters become inactive during periods of low food availability and it has been suggested that they remain in their burrows for up to three years if they cannot forage successfully--relying primarily upon fat deposits in their tails.

It is generally accepted that the venom of Gila Monsters functions primarily as a defensive weapon since eggs make up the bulk of their diet. Their bright or "warning" coloration supports this contention. Owls, Coyotes and Kit Foxes may be predators and there is one record of a young Gila Monster having been eaten by a rattlesnake. Man is by far the greatest enemy either through outright destruction of individuals or their habitat. Commercial collecting has also been a serious problem in some regions. For these reasons, the state of Arizona has proclaimed the Gila Monster as a fully protected species. Left alone in its habitat, an individual monster may live up to twenty years.

Gila Monsters are abroad both during the day and at night. They are most active in April and May when their chances of securing food are greatest. I have found them to be active at night during the summer rainy season in southern Arizona. In November they enter hibernation and are not seen on the surface again until March.

Breeding does not seem to occur in the spring as is the case with all other desert lizards. Rather, copulating adults have always been encountered in July or August. From three to five eggs make up an average clutch size though large females may lay up to twelve eggs. Presumably they are buried a few inches under the soil in an abandoned rodent burrow. About one month is required for incubation.

DESCRIPTION: The Gila Monster cannot be mistaken for any other reptile. Its black and orange pattern, beaded scales, swollen tail, and fourteen-inch length (excluding the tail) are distinctive.

DISTRIBUTION: Found in most habitats throughout its range. Common in areas with Saguaro Cactus and along washes at elevations from near sea level to 4,100 feet. Its range is limited to regions that receive several inches of rain during the summer months and have mild winters and hot summers. Thus it is essentially restricted to the Sonoran Desert of Arizona. Marginal habitat occurs in southern Nevada, extreme southwestern Utah and the eastern Mojave Desert as far west as the Clark Mountains of California.

Gila Monster, The Living Desert

Common Kingsnake (California) devouring a Glossy Snake

Common Kingsnake (Texas)

Common Kingsnake

This adaptable reptile is as much at home in irrigated farmlands as it is in rugged canyons or windblown sand hummocks. Yet localities where moisture is present, such as oases and desert streams, harbor them in greatest abundance.

A remarkable feature of Common Kingsnakes, Lampropeltis getulus, is their variability in color and pattern. In the Chihuahuan Desert individuals are black with yellow speckling. In portions of the Sonoran Desert they may be uniformly black. Throughout most of the desert areas of California and western Arizona kingsnakes are deep brown with white bands. A strikingly different pattern is found in an occasional specimen from Anza-Borrego Desert State Park in the extreme western Colorado Desert. Such a specimen may have a single white stripe running down its back. Banded individuals also live in the same region and it isn't surprising that for nearly 40 years herpetologists believed the two snakes to be separate and distinct species. But in 1936, Lawrence Klauber of the San Diego Zoo hatched both striped and banded kingsnakes from the same brood, thus proving the snakes were the same species. The differences were simply pattern variations like those found in many animals.

The kingsnake has the curious habit of eating its own kind. As a true cannibal, it may swallow any other smaller kingsnake. The victim could be a sibling or even its own offspring. This poses some interesting problems during springtime when a male and female get together for reproductive purposes. Fortunately, mating takes precedence over eating. There seems a tendency for this snake to be less inclined to swallow other kingsnakes during the spring months. An adult male kingsnake was once placed in a cage with a fourteen-inch longer female. As the month was April, the two snakes wasted no time in mating. After a few weeks as cagemates the male was removed to more spacious quarters. Several months later overcrowding in other enclosures necessitated that the two be reunited. Knowing how well the snakes got along, the keeper simply dropped the male into the cage with its mate. The next morning when the keeper returned, he was dismayed to find only one kingsnake, a very content and swollen female. Obviously, hunger had undermined the relationship as the female had devoured her mate!

Six to ten weeks following copulation, the female lays from four to fourteen pure white eggs which she deposits in an abandoned rodent burrow. Her sense of obligation ends at that point as kingsnakes, as well as most other reptiles, do not show interest in their young after egg laying. Life is hazardous for the newly hatched ten-inch young and it is the lucky kingsnake that reaches maturity. Busy highways, hungry birds of prey and adult kingsnakes are just some of the hazards awaiting them.

The name kingsnake comes from the propensity of these reptiles to devour other kinds of serpents including rattlesnakes. Such encounters usually take place at night in desert regions when predator and prey are searching for food. A kingsnake uses its tongue, in conjunction with other organs in its mouth associated with the sense of smell, to identify a rattler. Once located, the venomous serpent is doomed for the kingsnake immediately bites its victim and surrounds it with suffocating coils. The squeezing action is the same method used by the huge boas and pythons of the tropics, but in this case the prey is seldom killed. The tight loops prevent the rattlesnake from fully expanding its lungs and thus it is simply subdued through exhaustion. In such a state it is helpless to defend itself and is finally swallowed whole while still alive. Though the rattlesnake will struggle to free itself and may repeatedly bite the head and body of its foe, it is all for naught. Kingsnakes are immune to the venom. They prefer not to be bitten since lengthy fangs thrust deep into muscle tissue must be painful and can puncture the heart or lung. But this is usually avoided from the outset by securing a hold on the rattler's head.

Kingsnakes do not feed exclusively on venomous serpents. A coral, copperhead or rattlesnake will be eaten if not too large but these species are not necessarily preferred. Just as frequently birds and their eggs, small rodents, lizards and of course, harmless snakes are consumed. Size is probably the most important factor determining what food will be taken. Kingsnakes prefer smaller animals but have been known to swallow fairly large reptiles. There is an authentic record of a five-foot kingsnake swallowing a six-foot rat snake. This may seem an impossible feat but the kingsnake managed it by overlapping the victim into a U-shaped curve in its stomach. Needless to say, digestion of such large prey takes several weeks.

DESCRIPTION: Adults reach five feet in length and have patterns of white bands, yellow speckles or, rarely, a single, white vertebral stripe on a black or deep brown background.

DISTRIBUTION: Found throughout the Chihuahuan, Sonoran and Mojave Deserts. Also enters the southern Great Basin and extreme western Painted Deserts. Found in most habitats up to 7,000 feet.

These are active, fast-moving reptiles with pugnacious dispositions. When captured, they bite repeatedly causing painful but minor wounds as a result of their habit of pulling away before their teeth are free. The teeth break off and must be removed with tweezers. Such encounters are, at worst, a nuisance since whipsnakes possess no venom.

Countless times I have stumbled upon these snakes only to have them disappear within seconds into a burrow or dense vegetation. When trees are present they may escape by quickly traveling upward for ten or twenty feet. They appear to move very rapidly but in truth their top speed is less than half that of the fastest human. Their long, slender body ,and, in the case of some species, distinctive patterns, aid in the illusion of speed. The observer concentrates on the pattern and that image is impressed upon the retina. Then for a few seconds after the snake is gone, the eye continues to record that pattern. (The effect is akin to looking at a bright object and seeing the object even after we close our eyes.) Such a phenomenon can confuse a Road-runner or hawk just long enough to enable the whipsnake to escape. In addition, because of the multitude of shadows created by the stems and branches so often a part of the whipsnake's habitat, it is difficult to visually separate the snake from its background.

Whipsnakes, and the much rarer patch-nosed snakes (Salvadora spp., not discussed in the text) are the only strictly diurnal snakes found within the North American deserts. As one might expect, both maintain warmer body temperatures than other snake species, most of which are nocturnal, at least during warm weather. In fact, the thermoregulatory behavior of whipsnakes seems more akin to lizards. On a typical spring morning, they emerge from their burrow or crevice retreat at around eight and bask in the sun. When their body temperature reaches 86° F they start foraging. I usually encounter them between nine and ten in the morning or sometimes late in the afternoon about two hours before sunset. At these times, they are able to maintain their preferred body temperature of about 91° F. Only once in the past twenty years have. I found a whipsnake active at night. It was a recently hatched individual which wandered in front of my car at ten in the evening. Perhaps hunger or a drive to disperse from its place of birth drove it into this unusual behavior.

Whipsnakes forage primarily by sight. They frequently scout out the terrain by lifting their heads several inches off the ground. Should prey be seen, they move their heads from side to side, possibly as an aid to depth perception (see spiny lizards). Prey movement then attracts the whipsnake closer until a sudden rush catches the victim unawares. Prey is swallowed alive, quite unlike Gopher or rattlesnakes which kill their prey first. Larger victims are held to the ground with a loop of the body.

Whipsnakes are quite fond of nestling birds and I once had the opportunity of watching one search for them. I was camped in Organ Pipe Cactus National Monument and had set up my gear near a sprawling palo verde tree. As I had been sitting in my favorite camp chair, reading for nearly an hour, I was almost motionless. I happened to glance from the page and saw a four-foot-long whipsnake approach the trunk of my shade tree. It slithered up into the branches and seemed to know exactly where it was going. It headed straight for the nest of a House Finch. However, the nest was empty and upon determining this the snake moved directly through the tree to a Verdin's nest. It, too, was empty--the month being June and past the breeding season for most desert birds in this part of Arizona. I watched the snake crawl to the ground and head for a second palo verde some distance away. It found no food in that tree either.

In addition to nestling birds, whipsnakes are known to feed upon many other animals including small rodents, lizards and other snake species including small rattlers. Presumably they are immune to rattlesnake venom as is the kingsnake. Some insects are also consumed, especially sphinx moth caterpillars.

Desert Striped Whipsnake

Coachwhip

Mating occurs in April and the female deposits from four to sixteen eggs a few weeks thereafter. Within eleven weeks the eggs hatch giving forth pencil-girthed young about fifteen inches in length. The lifespan of whipsnakes in the wild is unknown but a captive individual is known to have lived almost seventeen years.

DESCRIPTION: Coachwhips (Masticophis flagellum) have a ground color which varies from pale orange to black, depending upon their place of origin. However, the braided-appearing tail and lack of a distinctive pattern should help distinguish this species. Both the Striped Whipsnake (M. taeniatus) and the Sonoran Whipsnake (M. bilineatus) have two or more stripes running the length of their body. All whipsnakes are long and very slender and may reach seven feet in length.

DISTRIBUTION: At least one of the three whipsnake species can be found in any particular desert habitat below 7,000 feet. All prefer open, sunlit areas. The Common Whipsnake is found throughout the North American deserts with the exception of the northern Great Basin Desert. It is rare in the Painted Desert. The Striped Whipsnake is essentially restricted to the Great Basin, Painted and Chihuahuan Deserts. The Sonora Whipsnake occurs in the central and eastern Sonoran Desert.

Gopher Snake

Young Gopher Snake emerging from egg

Gopher Snake

This is one of the most conspicuous and widespread snake species found in the North American deserts. It is an impressive animal--up to seven feet in length with a defensive display that can earn them immediate respect.

Many years ago I chanced upon a huge specimen some six feet in length with a wrist-sized girth. I wanted a closer look before it escaped down a rodent burrow and so hurriedly grabbed its midsection. To defend itself from such a large advesary, the snake curled back and imbedded its many pin-sharp teeth in my hand. I dropped the snake which hastily coiled and prepared to continue the encounter if need be. (Such wounds are not serious though they may bleed freely due to a component of snake saliva that retards clotting.)

Gopher Snakes are unique among reptiles of the West as they are capable of producing a loud and prolonged hiss when alarmed. The sound is produced by forcing air through the trachea, made unusually narrow because of the presence of a glottal keel, a structure unique to snakes of the genus Pituo-phis. My six-foot snake hissed continually, striking out at me whenever I got close. To the uninitiated, the Gopher Snake's large-blotched pattern, inhaling of air to expand its torso and habit of flattening the head during the defensive display suggest a rattlesnake. Should the snake be amongst dry leaves or grass the vibrating of the tail may even produce a noise that sounds like a rattle. This entire repertoire makes for an intimidating spectacle that must be an effective deterrent against enemies since most of the individuals I have encountered perform this display. Apparently many potential predators, and people, mistake Gopher Snakes for rattlesnakes and leave them alone. (It is interesting to note that Gopher Snakes from regions which are occupied by rattlesnake species that closely resemble them in pattern are most likely to imitate rattlesnake defensive behavior.)

Although desert-inhabiting Gopher Snakes may be abroad in the morning in early spring, they are primarily nocturnal from late spring through fall. Active snakes are searching for food or, should it be spring, mates. Rodents, including kangaroo rats, woodrats, ground squirrels, gophers, white--footed mice, rabbits, bird eggs and bats have all been recorded in the diet of these snakes. Young individuals also consume various species of lizards. Prey is killed by constriction. An individual snake throws powerful coils around the victim and squeezes it, preventing the lungs from expanding. Death results from suffocation. Gopher Snakes usually encounter rodents in their burrows and find them primarily through scent tracking. (A snake smells by constantly flicking its tongue which picks up minute particles that are transferred to "Jacobson's organ" in the roof of the snake's mouth.)

Like nearly all of our desert reptiles, Gopher Snakes enter hibernation during the late fall, finding some deep rock crevice or animal burrow in which to retreat. They are known to occasionally den with other snakes, including rattlesnakes and whipsnakes, and one such den in Utah contained over 400 individuals.

Breeding commences in spring, the female laying from six to thirty eggs six weeks after mating. Clutch size is dependent upon the size of the female and her health. Eggs are deposited in a vacated rodent hole as snakes cannot dig their own burrows. Within ten weeks, the seventeen-inch young are fully developed and break through the leathery eggshell.

DESCRIPTION: A tan, yellow or cream-colored snake with large brown or reddish-brown blotches. Individuals may reach seven feet in length.

DESCRIPTION: Found throughout all of the North American deserts, in most habitats up to about 8,000 feet.

Western Coral Snake - photograph by Howard Lawler

Western Coral Snake

Although it is related to the Indian Cobra, and its venom is about two times more toxic than that of most rattlesnakes, there are no recorded human deaths from the bite of a Western Coral Snake (Micruroides euryxanthus).

This fortunate situation is a result of several aspects of both its structure and habits. First, the species averages sixteen inches in length and has a very small head. Its front-mounted fangs do not fold back into the mouth when the jaws are closed as in the case of the rattlesnake, but rather are fixed and immovable. The fangs are thus necessarily short and the amount of venom small. Unless a coral snake has an opportunity to chew its fangs into human flesh, it is not likely to penetrate the skin. In addition, the openings through which the venom is injected lie further up on the hollow fangs than is the case with the rattlesnake. This requires that the coral snake imbed its fangs deeper into the tissue before venom can be injected beneath the top layer of skin.

However, as just mentioned, the venom is potent. It is neurotoxic in its effects causing rapid ascending paralysis and respiratory paralysis. Herpetologists Charles Shaw and Sheldon Campbell have concisely described the results of three instances where Western Coral Snakes had successfully injected venom into human victims.

"The symptoms, none of them severe, have been rapid and alike in all three cases. The victims felt pain at the immediate point of the bite, pain which continued from fifteen minutes to a few hours. Some hours after the bite each victim experienced drowsiness, nausea, and weaknss. All felt a tingling or prickling sensation, in one instance limited to the finger bitten, but in the other two cases spreading to the hand and wrist. In two of the cases symptoms disappeared within 7 to 24 hours after the bite. In the third and most severe case symptoms persisted for four days--and no wonder, for the 22-inch attacking coral snake was the largest ever recorded."

The habits of coral snakes also contribute to the scarcity of bites. It is a nocturnal species and, in addition, most likely to be abroad after warm, summer rains, periods when few people are outdoors. Coral snakes are also secretive, spending most of their lives under rocks or buried in the soil. In all of my wanderings through the Arizona desert over a period of two decades, only once have I ever encountered a coral snake.

No doubt the bright coloration of the Western Coral Snake serves as a defense mechanism, a kind of warning to predators that they are dealing with a dangerous serpent. If this fails, and an individual is continually disturbed, the snake buries its head among coils of its body and raises the tail to expose the underside. A most unusual act is then performed. The lining of the snake's cloaca is everted which results in a popping sound! Presumably this startles some predators giving the coral snake a chance to escape.

The powerful, neurotoxic venom of coral snakes is used to subdue their favored cold-blooded prey of small snakes and lizards. In captivity, they seem to prefer the tiny blind snakes found throughout their range. There are also records of them consuming shovel-nosed and black-headed snakes. One individual was found eating a small whiptail lizard.

Females lay two or three eggs in late summer which require about 2 1/2 months of incubation. The young are from seven to eight inches in length at hatching.

DESCRIPTION: This is a small snake from 13 to 22 inches in length, with a very small head, and girth seldom greater than a lead pencil. Wide red and black rings and narrow yellow or white bands completely encircle the body. (Although several other snake species "mimic" coral snakes by having similar colors, only the Western Coral Snake has red rings which are bordered by white or pale yellow.)

DISTRIBUTION: In the U. S., found in the Sonoran Desert of Arizona east to the extreme southwestern corner of New Mexico. Although the Arizona coral snake is found in a number of habitats from sea level to 5,800 feet, it is most frequently encountered in rocky upland desert where the Saguaro Cactus is common.

Sidewinder

No less than ten rattlesnake species are known to occur within the North American deserts proper. They range in size from the small, eighteen-inch Sidewinder (Crotalus cerastes) of the Mojave and Sonoran Deserts to the large Western Diamondback Rattlesnake (C. atrox) which has been known to reach over seven feet in length. Regardless of their size, all are venomous, dangerous, and should be given a wide birth if encountered.

Rattlesnakes can be active either during the day or at night, depending upon the temperature and time of year. In early spring, after emergence from winter dormancy, Speckled Rattlesnakes (C. mitchelli) are commonly encountered in the morning and afternoon. Daytime observations become increasingly scarce as summer nears and air temperatures exceed 90° F, the preferred body temperature of most rattlesnakes. During the summer months they forage at night.

One March morning, I discovered a male Western Diamondback Rattlesnake trying to prod a female out of large rodent burrow to mate. After nearly a half hour of his pestering, she finally emerged, and copulation ensued. The reproductive season is a springtime affair and is a time when male rattlers engage in "combat dances"--a kind of wrestling match where one male rears up and attempts to throw its opponent to the ground. The exact function of these rarely-observed events is not known but is thought to be a kind of territorial defense. Presumably the loser is driven from the area and is thus less likely to have the opportunity to breed with local females.

A second rattlesnake encounter occurred at Stubbe Spring in Joshua Tree National Monument where I had gone to take a look at a Bighorn Sheep water trough (called a guzzler). I saw no sheep but did find a large, three-foot Speckled Rattlesnake neatly coiled beside the trough, its concealing coloration making it difficult to spot. At first I thought it odd that it would station itself in such an exposed location but on close examination I saw that it had a feather protruding from the side of its mouth. Evidently this snake had snapped up a bird as it flew in to drink.

Although circumstances may occasionally result in a rattlesnake eating a bird, rodents are by the far the most important items in their diet. Pocket mice, kangaroo rats, woodrats, and ground squirrels are frequently preyed upon and the largest rattlers sometimes take cottontail rabbits. Small rodents are bitten and held whereas large prey are struck and then released. This minimizes retaliatory attacks which might injure a rattler. The snake follows and finds the mortally wounded mammal using its tongue and sense of smell to follow the prey's scent trail.

That rattlers can pinpoint the location of prey through use of their heat receptors is truly a wonder of nature. These receptors, called "loreal pits," are located on each side of a rattlesnake's snout. They detect subtle differences in the temperatures of objects by measuring the amount of heat or "infrared radiation" given off. So sensitive are they that differences of only 0.2° F can be detected. This high degree of sensitivity to temperature gradients enables rattlesnakes to precisely locate and strike their warm-blooded prey in complete darkness.

Rattlesnakes are ovoviviparous, a term meaning the eggs develop within the mother's body with the young snakes born alive. Two to twenty-five snakes make up a litter. The young have one rattle on their tail at birth and cannot make the rattling sound which gives this group its name. It is not until they shed their skin a second time that a second rattle is added. This permits them to make a small but audible warning buzz when danger threatens. A new rattle is added with each shedding. Rattlesnakes shed up to five times per year depending upon how much they eat, their health, and the temperature of their environment.

Each year nearly 1,000 people are bitten by rattlesnakes in the U.S. with 100 of these incidents occuring in Arizona. Approximately six to ten persons die as a result of the bites; a mortality rate of less than one percent. In 25% of the cases the rattlesnake does not inject venom. When venom is injected the seriousness of the bite depends upon a variety of conditions including the size and health of the victim, location of the bite on the victim's body, the size and species of rattlesnake, and the amount of venom injected. Elderly persons or those who are in poor health are more severely affected than young, healthy individuals. Likewise children or persons of small stature face a greater chance of serious complications since the ratio of venom to body mass is greater. In addition, large rattlesnakes are likely to inject more venom than small individuals and thus can inflict more damage. However, this generality must be qualified because the toxicity of the venom varies among species. For example, the venom of the Mojave Rattlesnake, Crotalus scutulatus, is sixteen times more potent than that of the Sidewinder. Venom of the Mojave Rattlesnake is the most toxic of any snake in North America so the bite of this species is of much greater medical concern. Knife blades and tourniquets aside (which in the hands of most people can result in medical consequences that are more severe than the bite itself), the best first aid advice is to get to a hospital as soon as possible. Regardless of the kind of rattler involved, a venomous snakebite is a serious medical emergency and requires immediate hospitalization.

DESCRIPTION: Blotched or diamond-shaped pattern on back, triangular-shaped head when viewed from above and, of course, rattles on the tail distinguish rattlesnakes from all other serpents.

DISTRIBUTION: At least one, and occasionally as many as six, rattlesnake species are found in any given region of the North America deserts. Most habitats are occupied.

Mojave Rattlesnake eating a pocket mouse

Valley of Fire State Park, Nevada

As a group, birds are recognized by everyone. Feathers and the ability to fly are obvious distinguishing features but their projecting beak, lack of teeth and egg-laying habit are also characteristic.

Unlike arthropods, amphibians, and reptiles, birds are "endothermic" which means they can burn up food energy fast enough to maintain a constant and elevated body temperature. Bird internal temperatures run from 104 to 108° F. By contrast, mammals, which are also endothermic, have body temperatures ranging between 98 to 100° F. In a hot environment a bird has an advantage over a mammal since there is less difference between the temperature of the air and the bird's body. The result is a reduction in the need to use up water for evaporative cooling. Birds do not sweat. Rather, when it gets too hot they keep cool through a kind of panting known as "gular fluttering." In this process birds flutter their loose throat skin which moves air rapidly over moist lung tissues.

Birds are also "preadapted" to desert life in that the waste product of their protein metabolism is uric acid which can be excreted as a semi-solid paste, rather than a liquid. Significant water savings are the result. The waste product of protein metabolism for mammals is urea which must be excreted in water.

Certainly the most dramatic advantage birds possess is their tremendous mobility. With the exception of the Roadrunner, birds can easily and rapidly fly several miles to waterholes. Many species also migrate out of the desert with the arrival of hot weather and breed in cooler, more humid environments. In some cases they may travel hundreds, even thousands of miles for this purpose. This strategy is unavailable to most other animal groups.

Turkey Vulture, Arizona-Sonora Desert Museum

Two species of vultures soar over the skies of the North American deserts. The Turkey Vulture, Cathartes aura, is the more common and widespread and, in the spring months at least, is seen throughout the northern as well as the southern deserts. The Black Vulture, Coragyps atratus, is confined to the Sonoran and Chihuahuan Deserts where it is somewhat less abundant than the Turkey Vulture.

Vultures are probably best known for their habit of feeding on rotting animal carcasses, a revulsive practice by human standards. However, scavengers like vultures play an important role in the environment by speeding up the recycling process that returns nutrients to the earth and by eliminating possible sources of disease. Vultures are protected from diseases associated with decaying animals by a sophisticated immune system that wards off disease-causing microorganisms and an unfeathered head that is easy to keep clean. Their "bald" head is distinctive and characteristic of vultures and condors throughout the world.

Vultures are of special interest to ornithologists because of their keen sense of smell, an attribute poorly developed in most birds. Field experiments have shown that Turkey Vultures can find rotting carcases without the aid of sight, and apparently over long distances. The area of the brain responsible for the sense of smell is much larger in vultures than in other birds of comparable size, suggesting an increased role of the olfactory sense. Of the two species of vultures in our deserts, it is the Turkey Vulture that seems to have the most highly developed sense of smell. Scientists have learned that the area of the brain involved in the discrimination of odors is three times larger in the Turkey Vulture than in the Black Vulture. Apparently Black Vultures rely more heavily upon sight to locate prey.

Although vultures typically feed on carrion, a captive vulture at the Arizona-Sonora Desert Museum killed a live Curve-billed Thrasher housed in the same enclosure. The thrasher was exhausted from battling a rival thrasher and was attacked by the vulture. Wild vultures also occasionally prey upon young or helpless animals.

Vultures obtain much of their water by feeding on moist carcasses. Water is, in turn, conserved as a result of their powerful kidneys which excrete high concentrations of nitrogeneous wastes resulting from the breakdown of protein. This enables them to use less water in expelling waste products.

Although Turkey Vultures migrate through all of the sub-divisions of the North American Desert, they breed only in the Great Basin, Painted, Chihuahuan and eastern Sonoran Deserts. Black Vultures breed just in the latter two desert regions. A cliff hollow is probably the preferred egg-laying site but no nest is built. Both parents participate in incubating the two eggs, an activity which lasts a little over one month. Newly hatched young are fed by regurgitation for the first few days. Within ten weeks after hatching the young fly from the nest.

DESCRIPTION: Featherless red head, six-foot wingspan, and silver-gray flight feathers distinguish the Turkey Vulture from other birds in the North American deserts. The Black Vulture is smaller with a five-foot wingspan, whitish patch on wing tips, and a dark, featherless face.

DISTRIBUTION: Large aggregations of Turkey Vultures, sometimes reaching several hundred, can be observed throughout our desert regions in late winter and spring as they migrate northward from Mexico. Within the North American deserts they are known to breed in the Great Basin, Painted, Chihuahuan and eastern Sonoran Deserts, while Black Vultures are restricted to the Chihuahuan and Sonoran Desert of Arizona.

Black Vulture, Arizona-Sonora Desert Museum

Red-Tailed Hawk

Large size, fierce appearance, and conspicuous flying habits combine to make the Red-tailed Hawk our most frequently seen bird of prey. Its five-foot wingspan and high, gliding flight make this species easy to spot against the daytime sky. In the North American deserts, the only other broadly distributed raptors which have larger wingspans are vultures and the Golden Eagle.

A Red-tail is usually observed while soaring in a warm updraft as it moves from one hunting perch to another. Effortlessly, it circles upward several hundred feet before gliding off to a new, elevated perch on a treetop or ridge. An adult hawk has superb vision and can spot objects that would be unobservable to a human from the same distance and vantage point. When a victim is sighted, the bird folds its wings tightly against its body and power dives at speeds up to 100 miles per hour. A sudden outstretching of the wings brakes the freefall and brings the hawk on top of its prey. The powerful talons quickly immobilize it.

For several weeks one spring I watched a pair of breeding Red-tails which had built a nest on a ledge atop a 65-foot vertical escarpment in Joshua Tree National Monument. It was totally inaccessible to non-flying animals, a nesting requirement of these birds. Other nest sites include the forks of cottonwoods, Joshua Trees and Saguaro Cacti, and the top of living or dead fan palms. Sticks, from ten to eighteen inches long, are the main ingredient used in construction. Although the pair I was watching had never used this site for nesting before, in most instances a nest is used through several breeding seasons. The same pair can be expected to use a nest since Red-tailed Hawks mate for life.

Incubation usually lasts 28 days but from my vantage point I could not determine when the eggs were laid. Only when the parents began bringing in food did I know the young had hatched. Two gangling heads, covered with white down, appeared above the rim in anticipation of being fed. Both had voracious appetites forcing their mother to spend most of the day away from the nest searching for food for her young as well as herself. Her return was always cause for much excitement. The male Red-tail was usually near the nest, watching over his offspring as well as his territory. Occasionally he would pitch in with the feeding chores but his efforts amounted to no more than 35% of the youngsters intake.

There are a few reports of three adults cooperating to incubate and rear a clutch laid by a single female. There may be one male and two females or two males and one female involved. It is not clear what circumstances lead to such an arrangement but the successful fledging of four chicks, instead of the usual two per nest, happens with much greater frequency when three adults are bringing in food.

All manner of living things comprise the diet of Red-tails. Lizards, snakes (including rattlesnakes), rodents, carrion and an occasional bird serve as food. Parents feed animals whole to their offspring or eat them first and then return to the nest. Upon arrival they regurgitate the contents of their stomachs, allowing the young hawks to feed upon the remains. Both parents and offspring obtain their water from the moist tissues of their prey.

I expected the youngsters I was observing to fledge in six weeks but that day never arrived. Two thoughtless men used the parents as targets and shot them both with 22-caliber rifles. The immature hawks perished on the ledge before park rangers discovered the assault. Most nesting failures, such as this one, are the result of human disturbances.

DESCRIPTION: The pink, red or orange tail (especially noticeable from above) and spotted breast band immediately identify this hawk. However, there is much variation and some individuals do not show these traits. Adults average eighteen inches from beak to tail though females are slightly larger than males.

DISTRIBUTION: Prefers to hunt in open areas but often nests in a concealed locality such as a ledge in a narrow canyon or fork of a cottonwood. Considered a resident throughout the North American deserts.

Red-tailed Hawk

Prairie Falcon

Prairie Falcon

The Prairie Falcon is one of the fastest creatures alive. Individuals have been clocked at speeds over 50 mph and some observers claim these desert falcons fly even faster; over 100 mph when diving from high above.

Regardless of how fast and powerful their flight, Prairie Falcons spend most of their time cruising over desert flats at moderate speeds and low altitudes. With rapid wing beats, these predatory birds skirt a few feet above the ground--a mode of travel ideally suited for sneak attacks on luckless dove or quail. A falcon suddenly appearing over a mesquite shrub at 30 mph surprises even the most wary animal. I have witnessed mixed groups of dove and quail leisurely feeding when suddenly a Prairie Falcon zooms into their midst scattering birds and feathers in all directions. The fruit of this labor is often a plump quail, one of the Prairie Falcon's favorite delicacies.

Prairie Falcons are adaptable birds, abandoning their low-flying sneak attack as occasion demands. One early spring afternoon while driving down a lonely desert highway a Prairie Falcon was seen flying in a queer zig-zag manner about sixty feet off the ground. This seemingly odd behavior lasted five minutes, the falcon constantly swooping within three feet of a shrub, then pulling out straight into the air. As we approached, the figure of a Round-tailed Ground Squirrel could be seen hiding beneath the bush, obviously in panic. The rodent was finally frightened into making a dash for its burrow--but it didn't quite make it. A lightning plunge by the falcon caught the squirrel dead in its tracks, the kill being made by the daggerlike talons.

As a bird of prey, the Prairie Falcon is unsurpassed in its ability to subdue other animals, sometimes even larger and more powerful than itself. The Great Horned Owl is nearly three times the size of a Prairie Falcon, yet this owl has been known to wind up as falcon prey. Great Horned Owls are slow fliers and sleep during daylight hours. Should a Prairie Falcon find one in an exposed location, the owl can become an easy target. In one eyewitness account a Prairie Falcon drove a Great Horned Owl into the open and repeatedly bombarded the confused bird with blows from its clenched talons. The owl was finally killed. In another instance a Prairie Falcon decapitated a Great Horned Owl with one blow. Although such observations are rare, they do reveal the aggressive behavior and power of the Prairie Falcon.

In addition to quail and an occasional owl, Prairie

Falcons feed upon a wide assortment of small animals including crickets, grasshoppers, reptiles and small birds and mammals. For some time ornithologists believed that Prairie Falcons did not consume snakes. However, an injured wild bird at the Desert Museum in Palm Springs readily ate snakes but only after it neatly removed the tough, scaly hide. So taken with the ease and precision with which the falcon handled the skinning operation, the researchers believed the bird was quite experienced in feeding upon serpents.

Although predators are often said to hunt only for food, the Prairie Faclon may stage mock hunts just for practice. Naturalist David Nunro observed a falcon which repeatedly flew nearly sixty feet upwards with an object clasped in its talons. Upon reaching that height, the object would be dropped with the falcon swooping down and catching it a few feet off the ground. If the object were missed, the falcon would pounce upon it after it hit the ground. Several times the bird grasped the "toy" in its beak and tossed it several feet away, only to jump on it again. Finally the bird tired of its game and flew off with Nunro hustling over to the site where the mysterious object lay. To his amazement, the toy turned out to be a piece of dried manure!

Prairie Falcons are most often observed during winter while ranging widely in search of prey. Common to many areas of the North American Desert, these birds are often overlooked as a result of their low-flying habits. During spring they become more localized in their distribution as males and females stake out territories. These territories are specific areas which provide ample food for both parents and offspring. By definition such areas are defended--even against human intruders should they enter the nest area. Nesting sites are usually quite inaccessible, high on some precipitous cliff face. Following mating, the female lays from three to six pink eggs, covered with numerous specks. Incubation time varies but normally averages thirty days whereupon the homely, down-covered young break through their shells. The youngsters are fed partially digested food until they can tear apart the animals left for them. The digested food is regurgitated by the parents who feed prior to returning to the nest. Although distasteful by human standards, regurgitation provides necessary moisture and an easily digested meal for the young falcons.

Even with the great care given the young, there is a high mortality rate in the first month of life. Nearly 35% of newly hatched falcons die during the first critical weeks. Fortunately, falcons that do make it out of the nest can mate before they are one year of age, and thus early breeding may partially compensate for high mortality.

DESCRIPTION: An attractive bird with bright yellow legs and feet, brown back, and white underparts with dark spotting. Average size ranges from seventeen to twenty inches from beak to tail with a wingspan of forty inches, placing it between the Red-tailed Hawk and the American Kestrel in size. When seen in flight from below, the pointed wings, long straight tail, light underparts, and dark axillars (junction of wing and body) are distinctive.

DISTRIBUTION: Found throughout the North American deserts. Prefers open areas. Some individuals breeding in the Great Basin and Painted Deserts migrate southward in fall.

Joshua Tree Woodland, Joshua Tree National Monument

Gambel's Quail, male far right, female far left, photograph by Hans Baerwald, courtesy Palm Springs Desert Museum

Gambel's Quail

One of the desert's most distinctive sounds is the call of the male Gambel's Quail. Once heard it is not likely to be forgotten. The four notes are slurred together and rise highest on the second note. The call carries for several hundred yards and functions to keep the flock or "covey" together and helps define territorial boundaries.

Although four species of quail are found in the North American deserts, the Gambel's Quail is the most abundant and widepsread. It ranges from portions of the Great Basin and Painted Deserts through the Mojave, and southeast into the Sonoran and Chihuahuan deserts. Individuals are known to occupy elevations below sea level in Death Valley and up to 6,000 feet in the pinyon and juniper forests of desert mountain ranges.

Gambel's Quail are most abundant in the vicinity of waterholes. In winter, when territorial aggression is reduced, huge coveys of over 100 individuals have been observed coming in to drink. Quail require drinking water if green, succulent vegetation is not available. This is the case in the summer months after the spring flowers have wilted away and during drought years when precipitation has been inadequate to produce new growth. Neither I nor other observers have ever found individuals more than one or two miles from the nearest waterhole.

Tolerance to dehydration has been demonstrated in quail. When deprived of water in captivity they have survived a 50% reduction in body weight as a result of water loss (although some of the reduction is assuredly a result of the metabolism of fat or other tissue). By comparison, the House Finch can withstand only a 27% reduction in body weight when deprived of water. Quail, as well as most other desert birds, can also reduce the rate at which they lose body water through evaporation. When not under heat stress, Gambel's Quail has a body temperature of about 104° F. But this rises seven or eight degrees when air temperature exceeds 104° F. By tolerating an elevated body temperature, these quail can delay the initiation of gular fluttering thereby conserving moisture through a reduction in evaporative water loss. (Gular fluttering is the process of vibrating the throat skin so that air moves rapidly over moist throat and lung surfaces. The evaporation of water from these surfaces cools the bird. It accomplishes what panting does for Coyotes, foxes, and some other mammals.)

Quail have numerous predators and thus time their arrival at waterholes so as to avoid an ambush. Studies have shown that quail drink primarily in the early morning and at dusk, the times when they are least likely to encounter hawks and falcons, their principal enemies. These predators visit oases from midmorning until midafternoon.

Traveling in coveys is another adaptation for dealing with predators. Nearly every desert hiker has been surprised by the sudden explosion of a covey of quail as individuals fly off in all directions. Such behavior can also startle and confuse a predator and prevent it from focusing its attack on a single individual. The net result is an enhanced prospect for each quail's survival.

Once, while walking up a desert canyon, I discovered a rather odd escape manuever used by very young quail. Although able to feed themselves from the moment of hatching, quail are unable to fly until they reach three weeks of age. Usually when danger approaches, young quail hide beneath shrubs or in rock crevices. However, in this instance no such cover was available and so the sixteen youngsters I was following rushed down rodent holes to escape me. They remained there for about four minutes, until their mother gave the all clear signal which caused them to emerge.

Breeding commences just before the time of year when food becomes plentiful. This is April throughout most of the North American deserts but occurs again in July in portions of the Sonoran and Chihuahuan Deserts in response to summer rains. Males and females pair at this time and establish their own nesting area. From ten to sixteen eggs comprise a clutch which is usually located on the ground. The female apparently does all of the incubating which lasts three weeks.

DESCRIPTION: The chunky, eleven-inch torso and short, rapid wingbeats distinguish quail from other birds. The male Gambel's Quail is identified by its white-outlined black mask and dark belly blotch. Both sexes have feather topknots.

DISTRIBUTION: Found from below sea level up to 6,000 feet throughout the North American deserts with the exception of the northern Great Basin Desert. Should be expected in most habitats though rare in areas of loose, windblown sand.

Doves are some of our most conspicuous and best known birds. The Mourning Dove (<u>Zenaida</u> <u>macroura</u>) is by far the most widespread species and breeds in each of the five desert regions. A second species, the White-winged Dove (<u>Zenaida</u> <u>asiatica</u>), has a much more restricted breeding range and occurs in lesser numbers in the Sonoran and Chihuanhuan Deserts from April through September.

Both species are dependent upon drinking water and unlike House Finches and Black-throated Sparrows, the doves' strict adherance to a diet of small, dry seeds force them to seek water throughout the year. However, the need to stay in the vicinity of springs, potholes and streams is somewhat ameliorated by their strong powers of flight. House Finches must stay within one mile of water during the hot summer months. Doves on the other hand may fly up to ten or more miles to reach water, greatly increasing the area available for foraging during the dry portions of the year. Doves are also unique among North American desert birds in that they drink by continuously sucking and swallowing, like a horse. Other desert birds dip their beaks into the water and then tip their heads back to allow the water to trickle down their throats. The former process enables doves to drink six times faster than other birds and significantly reduces the time spent at waterholes. This is an important adaptation since predators are known to frequently ambush their prey at drinking sites.

Both dove species may rear several broods during the course of their breeding season which lasts from March to October in the case of the Mourning Dove. It is the female that builds a nest consisting of sticks and dried grass arranged in a rather haphazard fashion. Frequently it is located in a cholla cactus but may also be placed on the ground or in a tree. Usually two eggs are laid which must be incubated for fifteen days. Both parents participate in egg incubation.

For at least the first few days, newly hatched doves are fed pigeon's milk, a liquid which is secreted from the lining of the crop (an enlargement of the esophagus) of both the male and female and regurgitated into the mouths of the nestlings. In addition to its nutritional value, this substance furnishes all the water the young birds require. By the time the young leave the nest, within two weeks after hatching, the parents have gradually changed the nestlings' diet to one of insects and seeds.

Although doves are strong fliers that can cover hundreds

White-winged Dove - photograph by Carol Davis

of miles in a single day and reach speeds up to fifty miles per hour, they must alight on the ground to feed and it is at this time that they are most vulnerable to predators. This was dramatically revealed to me when I witnessed the killing of a Mourning Dove by a Cooper's Hawk. The dove had been eating seeds scattered about my campsite when it suddenly attempted to fly off. The hawk seemed to appear from out of nowhere and struck with its talons just as the dove had taken to the air. The hapless bird fluttered on the ground a few seconds before the hawk struck a second time just five feet from where I sat.

DESCRIPTION: The 10 1/2-inch length, long tapered tail, and swift flight distinguish Mourning Doves from other doves and pigeons. As its name indicates, the White-winged Dove has white patches on its wings, the only dove with this characteristic. In poor light the relatively broad, rounded tail of the White-winged Dove, and slightly smaller size, can be used to distinguish it from the Mourning Dove.

DISTRIBUTION: The Mourning Dove is widespread, occurring in all of the North American deserts and in nearly every habitat. The White-winged Dove migrates into the Sonoran and Chihuahuan Deserts in late spring to breed, with the vast majority heading back into Mexico by the end of September. They prefer desert streamside habitats, wooded thickets and agricultural areas.

Mourning Dove - photograph by Hans Baerwald, courtesy Palm Springs Desert Museum

Roadrunner attacking a Sidwinder - photograph by Hans Baerwald, courtesy Palm Springs Desert Museum

The Roadrunner is one of our best known desert birds and also one of the most interesting. Its distinctive appearance, preference for running rather than flying, and ability to kill and devour rattlesnakes have helped instill an almost legendary reputation.

There are many exaggerated accounts of the running speed of Roadrunners but eighteen miles per hour is probably about as fast as one can travel. They prefer to run and only rarely take to the air since their short, rounded wings cannot keep their large bodies airborne for more than a few seconds.

Although not technically a "bird of prey," the Roadrunner feeds almost exclusively upon other animals. Rattlesnakes are the most notorious victims. On two occasions I have witnessed battles between these enemies and have come away in awe of the Roadrunners lightning fast reactions. The rattlesnake immediately coils when first confronted causing the Roadrunner to circle several times as it looks for an opening. The snake is coaxed into striking when the Roadrunner suddenly stops and lunges at it, with wings outstretched. This behavior functions to redirect the rattler's strike at the wing feathers rather than a vulnerable portion of its body. The strategy is akin to the use of a matador's cape. Each time the snake strikes, the Roadrunner springs into the air, always avoiding the lethal fangs. The rattlesnake opens itself up to a counter attack after striking and the Roadrunner is quick to take the offensive. With lightning speed it snaps the snake's tail up in its bill and, as though the snake was a whip, cracks it in the air. In one instance the Roadrunner was quick enough to catch the rattler's lower jaw in mid-strike. After several lashes the serpent tires and no doubt its vertebral column is damaged or even broken and it becomes helpless to defend itself. The Roadrunner is relentless and slams the hapless snake against the ground until it is dead. The entire battle rarely lasts more than five or six minutes and it seems the Roadrunner is always victorious.

I should note that a Roadrunner does not attack large rattlesnakes. Unlike hawks which tear their prey into bite-size morels, the Roadrunner must swallow its prey whole. Consequently, it prefers smaller animals that can be easily consumed. When engulfing snakes or lizards over nineteen inches long, portions are swallowed at intervals leaving a dangling tail hanging out of its mouth. Within an hour, the digestive process has created sufficient room in the Roadrunner's stomach to allow the remaining portion to be swallowed.

Although the securing of rattlesnakes as food is a dramatic spectacle, they are an uncommon item in the Roadrunner's diet. Insects and other arthropods are the dietary mainstay. Grasshoppers, ants, beetles (including Eleodes), and even such things as tarantulas, scorpions, and centipedes comprise the bulk of the food. Lizards are the second most important category of prey, followed by snakes of all kinds, rodents and birds. The speed by which these animals are captured is demonstrated by observations of Roadrunners snaring dragonflies and hummingbirds in midair.

The winter season may very well be the most difficult time of year for the Roadrunner. Reptiles are in hibernation, insects have largely died off and nestling birds have become agile adults or have migrated south. With the scarcity of animal food the Roadrunner is forced to consume some plant material such as the seeds or fruits of Sumac, cactus and Thornbush (Lycium). Up to 10% of its winter diet may be plant material. An adaptation that reduces the need for food energy is its habit of basking in the sun on cold winter days. The skin on its back is black and readily absorbs the sun's radiant energy when the Roadrunner reveals it by parting its feathers. Through using the sun's energy to keep warm rather than burning up food, a Roadrunner can reduce its caloric need by 41%, an impressive savings.

With the arrival of spring, a male Roadrunner not only captures food for himself, but also offers choice tidbits to a female as an inducement to mating. Typically, the male snaps up an insect or lizard and immediately rushes over to his mate. He may circle her a few times while she begs for the food. He quickly mounts her and their cloacas are brought together for a few brief moments. He then gives her the morsel. Sometimes nesting material is substitued for a food item.

This predictable courtship ritual serves to strengthen the bond between the adults; an adaptive strategy that ensures the male and female remain together to help raise the young. Both parents collect the small sticks that are used in nest construction. However, it appears that it is the female that actually builds the nest.

The clutch size is usually larger than the number of young that are reared. From two to twelve eggs have been found in nests and are laid up to three days apart. Half the clutches have one or more eggs that never hatch and often, some eggs are broken. Incubation begins when the first eggs are laid resulting in asynchronous hatching. The first to hatch crowd out the late hatchers and these "runts" may be eaten by the parents. Usually three or four young are finally fledged eighteen days after hatching. They stay in the vicinity of the adults for another week or two, and then disperse to surrounding areas.

Breeding adaptations have evolved to maximize the number of young that are produced. Thus in the Mojave and Sonoran Desert regions of California, where there is only a winter rainy season, Roadrunners nest in the spring; the only season when prey is sufficiently abundant to rear a brood. However in the Sonoran Desert of Arizona they breed again in August and September, taking advantage of a second season of abundance following the summer rains which occur in that region. In unusually wet winters Roadrunners may breed as early as January to take advantage of an expanding prey population or perhaps to produce two broods in one season.

Roadrunners show a number of behavioral and physiological adaptations to a desert existence. Certainly the most important is their carnivorous diet which provides them with an excellent supply of very moist food. They reduce evaporative water loss water through a 50% reduction in activity during the warm hours of midday. In addition, Roadrunners can reabsorb water from their feces before excretion, resulting in an additional savings. A nasal gland eliminates excess salt, a process that would require water if it were excreted through the urinary tract as it is in most birds.

DESCRIPTION: A large, mottled, black and white ground bird with a distinctive head crest. Males are indistinguishable in appearance from females. Twenty-two inches from the of the tip of tail to the end of beak.

DISTRIBUTION: Confined to open, flat or rolling terrain where large shrubs or small trees provide adequate nesting sites. Found throughout the North American deserts with the exception of the northern Great Basin Desert.

Burrowing Owl with grasshopper - photograph by Carol Davis

Owls are the nocturnal counterparts of hawks and falcons. Several specialized adaptations allow them to hunt at night including dense, soft feathers with ragged edges that give them almost soundless flight and enable a surprise attack. The forward-directed eyes possess retinas composed mostly of cones rather than rods, a feature that tremendously enhances nocturnal vision. The sensitivity of their hearing is legendary and several species can pinpoint the location of prey even without the aid of vision. This is facilitated by the owl's asymetrical ear openings. The ear openings occur on either side of the head with one located near the top and the other near the bottom. This increases the likelihood that sound waves will arrive at slightly different instances at each ear and helps owls better judge both the distance and location of the sound source. In addition, the facial disks of owls are composed of stiff, shallowly curved feathers which both intensify and direct sound to the ears and function much like a parabolic reflector.

With the exception of the Burrowing Owl among desert-inhabiting species, most female owls are larger than their male counterparts. Ornithologists believe this may function to reduce competition for food between the sexes, allowing females to attack larger prey. It may also enable the female to protect her young from the occasional cannabilistic tendencies of her mate.

Of the eight owl species known to breed in the North American deserts, only three are widespread and common: the Burrowing, Great Horned and Barn Owls. Of the three, only the Burrowing Owl (Athene cunicularia) can be observed during daylight hours for it frequently perches next to its burrow opening or on a nearby mound or low-hanging plant limb, often not retiring until midmorning.

The most distinctive feature of this latter owl is its burrowing habit. Although individuals seem to prefer enlarging a ground squirrel or tortoise hole to suit their needs, they possess the capability to construct their own underground retreat if necessary. Typically, the tunnels range from five to ten feet in length with the nest chamber lying about three feet beneath the surface. Considering the amount of diurnal and crepuscular activity of Burrowing Owls, their burrowing habit may be the single adaptation which enables them to exist in a desert environment. The one drawback of ground-nesting is that the eggs and young are vulnerable to predators such as rattlesnakes and Badgers. It appears Burrowing Owls compensate for increased predation by laying nearly twice as many eggs as do other owls.

Great Horned Owl - photograph by Hans Baerwald, courtesy Palm Springs Desert Museum

The Great Horned Owl (<u>Bubo</u> <u>virginianus</u>) is easily our largest nocturnal desert bird. Females are noticeably larger than males, weighing 2 1/2 pounds or 25% more than their mates. Both are usually detected by their hooting call which carries for up to a mile on still nights. They can often be brought in to a campsite by imitating the call. So long as there are trees, giant cacti or cliffs in which they can roost and nest, the presence of Great Horned Owls is assured. The female often lays her eggs in abandoned raven or hawk nests.

The Barn Owl (<u>Tyto</u> <u>alba</u>) is sometimes thought to avoid desert environments yet, with the exception of the Burrowing Owl, I see this species more frequently than any other. Perhaps with the development of so many towns and cities in the American deserts over the past few decades, suitable roosts in abandoned mines, dwellings, and groves of trees are always within close range. The Barn Owl is most frequently seen swooping in front of car headlight beams late at night.

With one exception, all of our owls breed in the spring. The Barn Owl breaks from this tradition and may breed at any time of year. This factor, along with a highly variable clutch size (three to eleven), enables Barn Owls to take advantage of temporary periods of abundant food. During prolonged droughts, when rodent numbers may be low, the clutch size is small and the last chicks to hatch may die of starvation. The reverse is true should a wet cycle ensue and rodents increase in number.

Any discussion of desert owls must include the world's smallest bird of prey, the Elf Owl (<u>Micrathene</u> <u>whitneyi</u>). Although it is more or less restricted to the ranges of the Saguaro and Cardon Cacti of the Sonoran Desert, when these cacti are present it is the most abundant owl. It nests in hollowed out cavities in these giant cacti, holes made by the Gila and other woodpeckers. At just five inches in length, it is about the size of a House Finch.

Competition for food resources among owl species that have similar tastes is usually avoided by hunting in different habitats or feeding on different prey items. For example, although both Elf and Burrowing Owls feed upon insects such as beetles, grasshoppers and moths, Burrowing Owls occupy open desert and agricultural areas where giant cacti are absent, thus avoiding competition with Elf Owls. This division may break down in the case of Great Horned and Barn Owls. Both feed on small rodents and it appears that where their

ranges overlap, considerable competition exists. Some ornithologists suspect that Barn Owls are replacing Great Horned
Owls around desert urban areas.

DESCRIPTION: The eighteen-inch height and feather
"horns" of the Great Horned Owl are distinctive. The
five-inch size and round head of an Elf Owl peering out from
a Saguaro cavity at dusk is not likely to be mistaken for any
other bird. The Burrowing Owl stands about ten inches in
height and is the only owl to be seen out on the ground in
broad daylight. The light, almost white color of of the Barn
Owl and its heart-shaped face are distinctive.

DISTRIBUTION: Most desert habitats in North America
sport at least one owl species. Great Horned Owls are
found throughout the North American Desert and occur over
every habitat. Elf Owls typically occur in those areas of
Arizona, Sonora and Baja California where the Saguaro and
Cardon Cacti occur. (Elf Owls are also frequently heard in
the pinyon woodland in Big Bend National Park.) Barn Owls
appear wherever manmade structures are found and any place
where dense stands of trees or narrow canyons are present.
They also utilize, and perhaps enlarge, hollows in earthen
banks of large washes or rivers. Burrowing Owls prefer open
habitats where tunnels can be constructed.

Elf Owl - photograph by Carol Davis

Hummingbirds are the smallest birds encountered in the deserts of the Southwest. In addition to their small size, they are characterized by long slender bills used for reaching deep into tubular flowers, incredibly rapid wingbeats that produce a humming sound, and the ability to fly backward--a feat no other bird group can duplicate.

During the day, hummingbirds maintain a high metabolic rate and therefore must feed frequently. However, on cool nights, they enter a state of torpor whereupon their temperature drops to that of the air, dramatically reducing their energy needs. This ability has enabled hummingbirds, an essentially tropical bird family, to enter our temperate desert regions.

Although a number of hummingbird species are known to migrate through the North American deserts, only three (Costa's, Black-chinned, and Anna's) are known to breed in arid regions and just one is truly associated with deserts. Known as Costa's Hummingbird, Calypte costae, this is the only species which reaches its greatest abundance in desert environments.

The male Costa's performs spectacular nuptial flights beginning in February, apparently to attract females. The aerial manuevers consist of hundred-foot U-shaped configurations accompanied by high-pitched sustained whistles. Such aggressive courtship behavior stands in marked contrast to the abandonement of the female after mating. Unlike many male birds which participate in nest construction, incubation duties and feeding of young, a Costa male plays no role after fertilization. A male may mate with several females and vice versa, a breeding system aptly termed promiscuous. The female lays two eggs in a tiny cuplike nest held together with spider webs, an excellent construction material for the webs expand as the growing young fill the nest. Only the female cares for the young.

Contrary to popular belief, young hummingbirds, and for that matter adults, are not reared exclusively on a diet of nectar. Insects and spiders are an important dietary mainstay and are essential for the growing young. Hummingbirds thus visit flowers not only for nectar, but also for the tiny arthropods which have entered the blossom. Occasionally, they can also be seen to capture insects in midair.

The most important behavioral adjustment of Costa's Hummingbirds is their exodus from the desert in late May and early June. There are almost no records of this species

Female Costa's Hummingbird and young - photograph by Hans Baerwald, courtesy Palm Springs Desert Museum

from June through September in Joshua Tree and Organ Pipe Cactus National Monuments, or for that matter anywhere in the deserts of North America. It appears that most of them migrate to the chaparral of the coast ranges of California at this time as their arrival there coincides with their disappearance in the desert. Several museum collections also harbor individuals with characterisitcs of Arizona populations but which have been collected in California during the summer.

It is not surprising that most individuals vacate the desert during the hot months. The small size of hummingbirds make them especially vulnerable to overheating. They must evaporate comparatively large amounts of water, through panting, to keep cool. It has been estimated that a 150-pound man would have to drink more than five gallons of water a day to maintain water balance if he lost water at the rate of a Costa's Hummingbird--and that's on a relatively mild day!

DESCRIPTION: Small size, long slender bills and rapid wingbeats distinguish hummimgbirds from all other desert birds. They are often aggressive and bold and sometimes dive at intruders, especially during the breeding season when males become territorial. The Anna's (Calypte anna), Black-chinned (Archilochus alexandri), and Costa's Hummingbirds are the only species known to breed in the deserts of North America. Males are distinguished by their purple (Costa's), black and lavender (Black-chinned) or reddish (Anna's) bibs or throats. Females are difficult to separate in the field.

DISTRIBUTION: Hummingbirds are most frequently seen around shrubs with red flowers such as the Chuparosa, Beloperone californica. Anna's is essentially a spring migrant and winter visitor in the deserts of California, Arizona, and Texas. The Black-chinned is chiefly a spring and summer resident in the Southwest. Costa's is the most tolerant of desert conditions and breeds in both the Mojave and Sonoran Deserts. Most Costa's leave for the California coast in late May but a few remain in the desert during summer.

Common Raven

Ravens

These large, black birds are among the desert's most conspicuous animals. Their loud call and labored flying across open skies assure their detection by even the most casual observers.

Carrion along roads and food scraps in campgrounds frequently attract ravens into situations where humans are near. However, their inability to become airborne rapidly and persecution as raiders of crops and domestic fowl result in their shyness when humans come close. Only in a few National Parks, such as Death Valley, Bryce Canyon, and Grand Canyon have I found them approachable.

Ravens are often confused with the much smaller crows. However, the latter birds are rare or absent in desert regions, usually travel in large flocks (not in pairs as do ravens) and possess a rectangular rather than a fan-shaped tail. The ravens weight of from 27 to 35 ounces makes them our largest songbird and nearly twice as heavy as a crow.

Ravens are omnivores but definitely prefer animal over vegetable foods. Biologist Lawrence LaPre' has observed a pair of ravens attack an adult rattlesnake on an exposed roadway and ravens are known to occasionally capture live rodents, lizards, insects and nestling birds. However, they are most often seen feeding on carrion and are commonly observed on roadways feeding on dead jackrabbits, snakes or any other animal that has met its demise under an automobile. It is not clear how ravens divy up such spoils with vultures which surely must compete with them since their ranges overlap in many regions. I have yet to see or hear of vultures and ravens feeding on an animal carcass at the same time and so must assume that one species drives the other away. In much of the Sonoran and Mojave Deserts vultures are absent except during spring and fall migration leaving the raven to scavenge alone. Unlike vultures, adult ravens are year-round residents in the North American deserts.

The jet black coloration of these birds has long puzzled scientists who are accustomed to observing desert animals that have evolved light fur, scales or plumages to reflect much of the sun's intense radiation (or to blend in with their surroundings). The very fact that ravens are widespread and reasonably common in our deserts tells us that this obstacle has been surmounted. Perhaps the extra heat gained in the cold winter months (and subsequent energy savings to the raven) is more important to the raven's survival than dealing with problems associated with summer heat. It is also important to remember that ravens have a tremendously broad and continuous distribution that includes mountain, forest and arctic environments. No significant color change occurs between any of these populations indicating that other factors, perhaps winter cold as mentioned above or species recognition, are of much greater importance in determining color.

Both parents participate in nest construction, a task that usually takes place upon a ledge on an isolated canyon wall. When the nest is complete, the female lays from four to seven eggs which take about three weeks to hatch. The male participates in both the incubation and feeding of the chicks which leave the nest within four weeks after hatching. One brood is raised per year.

DESCRIPTION: This is the only large, black bird that is likely to be seen flapping its way across the sky. The length of the Common Raven, <u>Corvus</u> <u>corax</u>, averages 24 inches. The Chihuahuan Raven, <u>C. cryptoleucus</u>, is smaller with a length of about 19 inches. The two ravens are difficult to distinguish in the field. Common Ravens from the southwestern deserts are somewhat smaller than individuals from more northerly latitudes.

DISTRIBUTION: The Common Raven is found over most habitats in all of the five subdivisions of the North American Desert. The Chihuahuan Raven, as its name suggests, is confined to the Chihuahuan Desert.

Curve-billed Thrasher - photograph by Carol Davis

Relatively large size, preference for running and active foraging habits make thrashers fascinating to watch. On countless occasions I have observed LeConte's and Curve--billed Thrashers use their long, downward-curved bills like rakes and hoes to uncover insects beneath surface litter. Sometimes they make quite a commotion and have been known to dig holes two or three inches deep in their quest for some delectable beetle grub or moth larva.

Five species of thrashers are found in the deserts of the U. S. The Crissal Thrasher (Toxostoma dorsale) is the largest but also the least seen. It inhabits dense stands of mesquite and other shrubs, immediately running for cover when disturbed. Although all of our thrashers are essentially ground-dwelling birds, the Crissal is the most terrestrial and usually escapes danger by running.

By way of contrast, the Sage Thrasher (Oreoscoptes montanus) is the smallest of the five and is more likely to avoid intruders by flying. Individuals are observed as often above the ground, perched in a shrub or flying, as they are running on the surface. Their habit of breeding on the sage-covered flats of the Great Basin Desert in late spring and summer means they must migrate south into the lower deserts during winter where the climate is less harsh and food resources are more readily available.

Bendire's Thrasher (Toxostoma bendirei) also migrates southward as fall approaches, but since its breeding range does not extend into the cold Great Basin Desert, the distances individuals must travel to reach the relatively mild-wintered environments of the Sonoran and Chihuahuan regions is not nearly so great. As is true of several members of the bird family known as Mimidae (which includes the well-known mockingbird) Bendire's Thrasher is known for its varied songs and calls.

LeConte's Thrasher (Toxostoma lecontei), more so than any other member of this family, is found in very arid habitats. Its pale color mirrors the terrain, which it runs over with surprising speed. I usually first detect an individual by its single, upward-pitched call, similar to that of the Phainopepla.

The Curve-billed Thrasher (Toxostoma curvirostre) is probably the most common and certainly the most conspicuous species in the group. It would be a rare day that this species is not recorded in a birdwatcher's notebook when traveling in Saguaro country. The Curve-bill occupies the same cactus-covered flats that the Cactus Wren prefers. Since they both roost and nest in cholla and feed on small arthropods, seeds, fruits and occasional small lizards, it's not surprising that confrontations take place. Except when defending its nest, the smaller Cactus Wren always retreats rather than fight. A Curve-bill also seems to enjoy tearing up wren nests whenever the opportunity presents itself. This may function to depress the numbers of Cactus Wrens in an area and thus reduce competition.

Nesting and breeding begin in spring. With the exception of the Sage and Crissal Thrashers which nest in shrubs such as mesquite, most thrasthers prefer to nest amongst the dense spines of cholla cactus. From two to four speckled eggs are laid in a cuplike nest in contrast to the covered nests of the Cactus Wren. Incubation lasts about fourteen days. All of the young leave the nest within eighteen days after hatching. In southern Arizona, the Curve-billed Thrasher has been known to lay up to four clutches and successfully fledge three families. However, in Saguaro National Monument the average fledging success is about 1.2 broods for each mated pair of thrashers. Interestingly, Gambel's Quail, Abert's Towhees, and both Mourning and White-winged Doves are known to occasionally lay their eggs in abandoned thrasher nests.

DESCRIPTION: Down-curved bills and habit of running with tail erect are distinguishing features of these birds. To separate the five species of thrashers found in the southwest deserts it is often necessary to look carefully and observe the following characteristics. (1) The Sage Thrasher is small (7 inches long), has a relatively short bill and a streaked breast. (2) Bendire's is somewhat longer (8 1/4 inches) but it too has a short bill. Fortunately for birdwatchers, its breast is faintly, not markedly, streaked as is the Sage's. (3) The red-orange eye color and dark tail of the Curve-billed usually separate it from other thrashers. (4) The large size (10 1/4 inches) and rust-colored undertail of the Crissal are distinctive. (5) The pale color of the LeConte's Thrasher stands in marked contrast to its dark tail.

DISTRIBUTION: All of our desert thrashers prefer shrubby areas and some flat ground for running. At least one of the five species discussed in this section is found in each of the five subdivisions of the North American Desert. (1) During the summer months look for the Sage Thrasher on juniper and sagebrush flats of the Great Basin and Painted Deserts. During the winter it is widespread but prefers dense shrubbery in the Sonoran and Chihuahuan Deserts. (2)

Bendire's Thrasher is most common where arborescent cacti are present but its range extends well into the juniper country of the Painted Desert. (3) Curve-billed Thrashers are common in the Chihuahuan and Sonoran Deserts east of the Colorado River, wherever arborescent cacti or dense shrubs are abundant. (4) Crissal Thrashers are found in areas of dense thickets along riparian corridors and along densely vegetated washes in the Sonoran, Chihuahuan and to a lesser extent the Mojave Deserts. (5) LeConte's Thrasher is uncommon in arid shrublands from the southern Great Basin through the Sonoran Deserts.

LeConte's Thrasher

Cactus Wren - photograph by Carol Davis

Although the presence of many bird species is first determined by seeing them, the Cactus Wren (<u>Campylorhyn</u>-<u>chus brunneicapillus</u>) is usually heard before it is seen. Both sexes indulge in an array of vocalizations used to communicate their location and emotional state. The most distinctive call is a kind of incessant, sharp-noted staccato that nonaficionados might kindly describe as irritating. But to desert enthusiasts, the early morning call of the Cactus Wren announces that all is well in the cactus-covered landscapes preferred by these birds.

As its name might suggest, the Cactus Wren prefers to build its nest in cacti. In fact the spinier the cactus the better. Species of cholla seem preferred and anyone who has ever had cholla spines imbedded in their skin knows the protection afforded the wren's nest. (The spines have backward pointing barbs that affix themselves harpoon-style into an animal's flesh.) Many predators that feed on young birds are dissuaded from attacking Cactus Wren offspring because the wren's nest is surrounded by spines.

Of course the wren must avoid these same spines, a feat it usually accomplishes without much difficulty. However, on at least one occasion I have found a young wren impaled on the spines and Wes Weathers of the University of California has observed adults pulling spines from their feet with their bills. These are rare events to be sure and the tradeoffs weigh heavily in favor of a cactus-inhabiting lifestyle. The abundance and widespread distribution of the Cactus Wren attests to this fact.

Cactus Wrens are unique among birds in that a pair builds several nests within their permanent territory of from one to ten acres. Early naturalists believed these nests functioned as decoys to frustrate predators that might crawl into a cactus plant, animals such as Gopher and Common Whipsnakes. But studies by Ander and Anne Anderson showed these nests functioned mostly as shelters to protect against extremes of heat and cold. One nest is used to lay the eggs which number from four to five per clutch. A second nest is used by the male as sleeping quarters. A third may provide fledglings with shelter. Both male and female construct the nest in which the eggs are to be laid, but either sex may build secondary nests alone. Nests are pouch-shaped with a hole leading into the center.

A female lays her first clutch of the spring approximately eighteen days following copulation. She alone incubates the eggs, a chore which lasts sixteen days. Young fledge in twenty-one days.   Up to three broods may be fledged in a single year.

Cactus Wrens have insatiable curiosities.   They are constantly searching out insects; by probing into crevices, scratching at the ground or turning over surface objects. Being quite bold, they become accustomed to the presence of humans and are often easy to view close up.   In campgrounds they jump down into trash cans and begin tapping the sides and bottom trying to loosen some morsel of food.   When disturbed at this activity they hop out of the can and scold the intruder with loud squawking.

I once set out a live trap to detain a ground squirrel but to my surprise captured a Cactus Wren instead.   It had gone into the trap for the grain I had used as bait and was not at all pleased with its detainment.   About 20% of the Cactus Wren's diet is plant material.

DESCRIPTION: This is our largest wren reaching almost nine inches in length.   Spotting on the breast and distinct white stripe over the eye distinguish this species from other wrens.

DISTRIBUTION: Found throughout the Chihuahuan, Sonoran and most of the Mojave Deserts, wherever shrub or tree cacti occur.   In addition to cacti, Cactus Wrens occasionally nest in acacia and palo verde.   To find them, listen for their call and look for their grass and twig oval nests in shrub and tree cacti.

Phainopepla

There are several reasons why this species is one of our most interesting desert birds. First, although Phainopeplas (Phainopepla nitens) breed in the desert they can't be considered residents since they disappear from it in summer. Second, Phainopeplas grow their own energy needs by inadvertently "planting" mistletoe seeds. Finally, like ravens, male Phainopeplas are jet black, a color which absorbs more heat than any other--seemingly a poor adaptation for a desert animal.

Flocks, some of which contain thirty or forty Phainopeplas, return to the desert in October when high daytime temperatures start to decline. Males establish territories around patches of mesquite or palo verde that are parasitized by mistletoe. The fruits of the mistletoe provide both nourishment and moisture and comprise the bulk of the Phainopepla's winter food in many regions. However only the flesh is actually digested with the seeds passing out unharmed. Seed-laden droppings accumulate on mesquite branches lying beneath perches and eventually a seed succeeds in germinating and pushing its rootlet into a mesquite stem. Ultimately, the new mistletoe plant produces berries that will be eaten by Phainopeplas, as well as some other species of desert birds. Flying insects are also eaten and captured in midair. This latter food resource is especially important during the spring and summer when nestlings require a diet high in protein.

Courting activities begin as early as January and can last until May. One of the first indications of the breeding season is the male's nest building activities. Nest construction is his responsibility alone and if his creation is satisfactory a female takes up residence in his territory. She lays from three to five speckled eggs and the young fledge within five weeks after her last egg is laid. By the end of April all young have left their nests and it is at this time that the Phainopeplas mysteriously vacate the desert until the following October.

For many years it was not clear where they went. However researchers now know that Phainopeplas travel to less stressful climates at higher elevations or along the southern California coast. In these localities a second brood is raised making the Phainopepla the only bird to nest in two entirely different environments within a single season. They utilize the mild climate of the warm Sonoran Desert during winter, nest in early spring when a burgeoning insect population is available for their young and then vacate the desert during the most stressful months of summer.

Since Phainopeplas leave during the summer months when solar radiation is most intense, their black coloration should be less of a handicap than that of the raven which is a year-round resident.

DESCRIPTION: The red-eyed males are all black with white wing patches that show during flight. Females are gray with paler wing patches and brown eyes. Both sexes have head crests. A short, soft whistle characterizes their call.

DISTRIBUTION: Found throughout the Mojave, Sonoran and Chihuahuan Deserts, wherever mistletoe grows.

Phainopepla (male) - photograph by Jan Zabriskie

Although much smaller than any of our hawks or falcons, the Loggerhead Shrike (<u>Lanius</u> <u>lucovicianus</u>) is equally ferocious and is, in practice, a bird of prey. Grasshoppers, crickets and beetles are their normal food but I have seen them capture lizards on many occasions and once observed a young House Finch killed by a shrike's powerful bite. Even small mammals such as pocket mice and young ground squirrels are known to be victims and Mourning Doves, nearly three times the size of a shrike, may occasionally fall prey. Their depredations are so systematic that during the spring breeding season, shrikes may decimate local populations of nestling birds.

As a passerine (the order of birds which includes sparrows and finches), shrikes do not possess the powerful talons of true birds of prey and, therefore, one might think their small feet would put them at a competitive disadvantage. However, they partially compensate for this deficiency by carrying prey in their bill during flight and by using spines and thorns on which to impale their victims. So affixed, small pieces can be torn off and easily swallowed. Shrikes often return to feed at these stations if they are not able to consume the entire animal at one feeding.

Shrike nests are located in open habitats where there are good lookout perches from which to hunt. I have even found nests in sand dunes so long as there were a few large Creosote Bushes in the vicinity. Nesting is accomplished in March or April, the female laying from four to seven white, spotted eggs. Breeding territories average about twenty acres.

The tables may be turned on shrikes when Roadrunners are in the vicinity. Shrikes are not fond of Roadrunners, especially during the breeding season. Apparently, these latter birds may steal shrike young as the mere sight of a Roadrunner in the vicinity of their nest sends a shrike pair into a frenzy. That is why I was surprised when I once found a shrike nest situated within fifteen feet of an active roadrunner nest, in adjacent palo verde trees. I watched them for about an hour and discovered that they resolved this apparent dilema simply by ignoring each other. Each species would enter its respective nesting tree on the side furthest from, and out of view of, the other's nest. This strategy seemed to eliminate temptation and permitted a temporary peace.

Loggerhed Shrikes show no unique adaptations to desert living. Although they may hunt during the hot hours of midday, they utilize shaded perches while waiting for prey to appear. Apparently they remain within their territory throughout the year and do not visit water holes. As carnivores, so long as they have sufficient food they are able to remain in good water balance.

DESCRIPTION: At first glance shrikes resemble mockingbirds because of their white underparts, dark wings and white wing patches. However shrikes can be distinguished by their short hooked bill, stocky heads and bodies, and black mask. Both birds are from nine to ten inches in length.

DISTRIBUTION: Found in all open habitats throughout the North American deserts so long as there are at least a few large shrubs. Absent from canyons.

Loggerhead Shrike, The Living Desert

Black-Throated Sparrow

These attractive sparrows are less dependent on drinking water than any other seed-eating bird. Even during the hottest days of summer, on Creosote-covered flats far removed from springs, they can be found when every other granivorous bird has vacated the area.

Their success is not due to any unusual capacity to tolerate heat or dehydration. On the contrary, Black-throated Sparrows (Amphispiza bilineata) are like most other birds in these respects. Their secret is a change of diet, substituting moist insects for seeds during the summer months. In addition, since they can tolerate saltier water than can House Finches and doves, certain drinking sites may be of benefit to them but not to other avian species. When deprived of drinking water, Black-throated Sparrows also conserve moisture by dehydrating their excreta from 81 to 57% before discharge. A final adaptation is their habit of seeking refuge in rodent burrows on exceptionally hot days.

With cooler temperatures in the fall, these sparrows resume their granivorous habits, supplemented with bits of green vegetation produced after the first winter rains. Although laboratory studies have shown that they can survive without water on a diet of dry seeds, they can accomplish this only when temperatures are cool. Hot spells during spring or fall, drive Black-throated Sparrows to waterholes because they are eating mostly seeds at these times of year.

Breeding activities begin as early as February, but usually start in March. Up to four egg clutches may be laid, although no pair probably raises more than three broods by the end of the breeding season in June (this is at least one more clutch than is laid by any other small, granivorous bird). An average-sized clutch consists of three or four eggs. One reason for the large number of clutches may be to compensate for the higher-than-normal predation of the eggs and young. Black-throated Sparrows construct their nests in dense shrubs within a foot of the ground. The young are thus vulnerable to a wider range of predators, such as snakes and rodents, than are other bird species. There are, however, several advantages to this strategy. Shrubs are the most abundant growth form in deserts and so there is no shortage of suitable nesting sites. In addition, should nestlings fall out of the nest, they are less likely to be hurt and can continue to receive parental care. Finally, dense shrubs provide abundant shade, an important consideration in a desert environment.

On hot days in spring, parents become inactive to avoid producing any unnecessary metabolic heat. They remain in the shade and, if necessary, hold their wings outstretched to block any sunlight that might strike the nestlings.

DESCRIPTION: Males and females are identical in appearance with a black throat, two white face stripes, a five-inch length and weight of approximately one-half ounce.

DISTRIBUTION: Found in all desert habitats from below sea level to 6,500 feet. Most common on rocky slopes where Ocotillo and succulents abound. Scarce above 3,900 feet. Considered a resident in the Chihuahuan, Sonoran and Mojave Deserts. Found in the Great Basin and Painted Deserts only during the summer breeding season.

Black-throated Sparrow adult (right) and immature (left)

House Finch

This is our most abundant and widespread desert bird. During one spring, no less than eleven occupied nests were found within two acres in California's Joshua Tree National Monument, the highest breeding density of any desert bird of which I am aware.

House Finches, _Carpodacus mexicanus_, are most conspicuous near springs and waterholes, especially during the hot summer months when their need for moisture is greatest. In some cases they may fly several miles to reach these drinking sites. Unlike rodents which can conserve water by going underground, House Finches, as well as most other birds, remain topside and thus use large amounts of precious water for evaporative cooling. It is true that they minimize the amount of water they lose by confining their activity to the early morning hours and at dusk, and by remaining in the shade whenever possible. But seed-eating birds still must have water to drink to replace that which is lost through evaporation.

Although occurring in most desert habitats, the House Finch is found in greatest concentrations at low elevations. During the winter months they form large flocks, sometimes numbering several hundred individuals, which travel about in search of small seeds on which to feed. In spring, these flocks break up as breeding pairs are formed and territories established. In wet years two or more broods may be raised. Both parents participate in building the open-cupped nest which is usually located in a branching shrub with thorns or spines. In desert habitats, cacti and leguminous trees are preferred. A typical clutch consists of four or five eggs which must be incubated for fourteen days. Both parents participate in incubation. The young fledge within sixteen days.

During the fall and winter months, other similar-appearing finches may move into the North American desert region, especially if unusually harsh winter conditions prevail in the mountains. The Purple Finch, distinguished by its lack of dark streaks on the side of its belly (male) and white line behind the eye (female), usually appears in very small numbers in all but the Chihuahuan Desert. Cassin's Finch, also with unstreaked sides but with a red crown that contrasts markedly with a brown hind neck (male), is a very rare visitor to the desert lowlands in winter and is occasionally seen in the higher desert mountains during spring. These two finches are often overlooked because they so closely resemble House Finches, especially the females. Binoculars and a little patience will help separate these three closely related species. By April, the few Cassin's and Purple Finches have left for their mountain breeding haunts, leaving the deserts entirely to the House Finches.

DESCRIPTION: The reddish head, breast and rump of the male distinguish this 5 1/2-inch bird from all other desert species. In some male individuals the red is replaced with yellow or orange, a condition thought to result from a dietary deficiency. The female lacks the red and can be difficult for the novice to identify if she is not in the company of a male. The streaked breast, stubby bill and lack of eyestripe can aid in female recognition.

DISTRIBUTION: Observed in most desert habitats, from Creosote or cactus-covered flats into the Pinyon-juniper Woodland. Most abundant near water. Occurs in all of the North American deserts.

House Finch (female)

Mammals are characterized by the possession of body hair, different types of teeth for different functions, and mammary glands that produce milk for the nourishment of their young. The fertilized eggs of mammals develop within the body of the female as compared to the external development within the shelled eggs of most amphibians, reptiles and birds.

With only a few exceptions, most desert mammals are nocturnal and this is their chief water conserving strategy. Most also seek shelter in burrows and those which do not, with the sole exception of the jackrabbit, must have regular access to drinking water or feed on exceptionally moist food.

Cactus forest in Organ Pipe Cactus National Monument. Gila Monsters, Cactus Wrens, and Collared Peccaries occur in this habitat.

Western Pipistrelle - photograph by Robert L. Leatherman

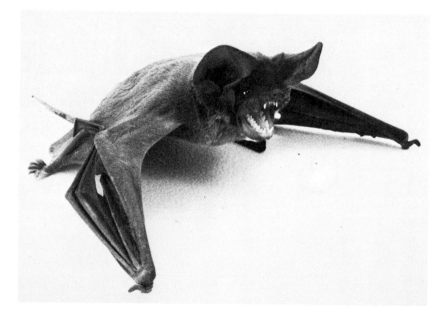

Brazilian Free-tail Bat - photograph by Hans Baerwald, courtesy
Palm Springs Desert Museum

Bats (about 850 species) are second only to rodents (about 1,760 species) as the most abundant group of mammals. At least 27 different kinds of bats are known to occur in the North American deserts representing both nectar and insect-eating species. The largest, the Western Mastiff Bat (Eumops perotis), measures 22 inches from wing tip to wing tip compared with the smallest, the Western Pipistrelle (Pipistrellus hesperus), which is just one third that size.

Bats are, of course, mammals and though they may seem quite unlike dogs and cats they possess all of the mammalian attributes. Every species has fur, a warm body temperature, gives birth to young which are not enclosed in an egg, and produce milk from mammary glands. Just one or two young comprise a litter and in some species newborn bats may ride with their mother during nighttime foraging.

Popular beliefs about bats are often exaggerated or misconstrued. They are commonly depicted as direful creatures of the night that suck blood, become entangled in human hair and transmit rabies. Vampire bats do drink blood which they lap from wounds made by their bites. But the species which is known to attack humans is not found in the deserts of North America, occurring only as far north as central Mexico. (There is one species of bat which occurs in the Big Bend area of western Texas that does feed on the blood of birds.) I have never heard of anyone having a bat become entangled in their hair. Bats have a superb echolocation system that enables them to detect the precise whereabouts of any object, even tiny flying insects. They're not going to purposely collide with someone's head. It has been estimated that about one in a thousand bats carries rabies, and these ultimately die from the infection. Ten human deaths in the U.S. have been reported. Obviously, sick or injured bats should never be picked up.

The vast majority of bats are quite harmless. In fact they are of tremendous benefit. For instance, some species play a vital role in plant reproduction. Hognose (Choeronycteris mexicana) and Longnose Bats (Leptonycteris nivalis) are important pollinators of the giant Saguaro Cactus. Insectivorous species, such as the Western Pipistrelle, eat vast quantities of moths, flies and beetles and help maintain a check on the populations of these insects. At Carlsbad Caverns National Park in New Mexico, nearly one million Brazilian Freetail Bats, Tadarida brasiliensis, emerge each summer night to begin their search for prey. If each bat captures ten insects, that's a total catch of ten million every night. And that's just in one small area. Obviously the ecosystems of the North American Desert would be dramatically altered if bats were to suddenly disappear. (The Carlsbad bat population has dropped significantly during the last thirty or forty years. The population plummeted concurrently with the use of DDT in the cottonfields of New Mexico and west Texas.)

Old buildings, rock crevices, cottonwood trees, abandoned mine tunnels and, of course, caves serve as daytime roosting sites. While "sleeping" most species allow their body temperature to drop, as do hummingbirds, and go into a temporary state of torpor. This conserves energy that would otherwise be used just to keep warm. (The trick, of course, is to find a safe hiding place since a bat cannot escape a snake or some other predator while in torpor.) Though essentially nocturnal in their habits, some species emerge from these roosts in the late afternoon, especially in the early spring when nights may still be cold. Most species return to rest around midnight and then forage a second time in the early morning hours. Occasionally I observe Western Pipistrelles still hunting one or two hours after sunrise.

It is the desert's winter cold, and accompanying scarcity of insects, not the summer heat that is the most difficult environmental obstacle for bats. Most bats therefore hibernate during the winter while a few species migrate south into Mexico. Nevertheless, the occasional squeaks heard on cold winter nights indicate that some bats are active. This is surprising since their small size causes them to lose heat rapidly, espcially as they move through cold night air, and few insects are available as food. Part of the answer to this puzzle is that bats flying during winter may not be maintaining a normal body temperature of 100° F. One study revealed that bats can fly with a body temperature as low as 73° F. Such a lowered metabolic rate would significantly reduce the amount of energy needed to maintain a "normal" body temperature. But why fly if insects are not available? The small size of most bat species facilitates dehydration and, unlike rodents, they are not able to secure a refuge that is as humid as an underground burrow. Thus it may be that nighttime flights during winter are to obtain drinking water.

Sounds made by bats as they fly through the air function to guide them through their habitat and to secure prey. The sound waves bounce off objects and return to the bat's ears. Size, composition, and distance of each object can be assessed with incredible accuracy through use of this echolocation technique. (Bats do not capture insects in their mouths as do some birds. Rather they use the membrane of their wings and tail to "basket-catch" prey. Only after capture, and while still flying, do they reach back and bite, kill and swallow the victim.) If one listens carefully on a warm summer night individual bats can be heard as they emit calls which are audible to humans. These sounds are usually to communicate with other bats. Ultrasonic sounds are inaudible to humans and are used to locate prey.

Animals closely synchronize their breeding cycles so that the young are born at the most favorable time of year. Scientists were thus surprised to discover that many bat species breed in the fall, just before the onset of winter. At first this seemed to be maladaptive as the gestation period for such small animals should be short resulting in the young being born in late fall or even winter when few insects are about and temperatures are low. However, it was discovered that fall mating species are hibernators and that in certain cases the fertilized eggs do not immediately implant into the uterine wall of the female. Instead the eggs only develop to the blastocyst stage and then become dormant while the female hibernates. Once the female becomes active in the spring, the blastocyst implants and begins to develop normally. The end result is that the young are born in late spring, the most favorable period of the year. This phenomenon is known as "delayed implantation" and has evolved in some weasels as well. Other bat species achieve the same result through delayed fertilization. In this phenomenon, male sperm cells become dormant in the female's uterus until early spring when ovulation and fertilization occurs.

Bats may be surprisingly long-lived. While most mammals the size of bats (from 0.3 to 1 ounce) live for a year or less, bats live for periods ranging from four to thirty years. Bats that are active all year may have an average life span ranging from four to seven years. But some small hibernating bats have been shown to live for periods ranging from 25 to 30 years. In comparison, a shrew of comparable body weight may live for only six months.

DESCRIPTION: Bats are not likely to be confused with any other mammalian order. They are the only mammals which can truly fly. Their wings are composed of skin stretched between the bones of the arm and the greatly elongated fingers.

DISTRIBUTION: Twenty-seven species of bats inhabit the North American deserts. No habitat is without at least two of these species.

Spotted Skunk - photograph by Robert L. Leatherman

Striped Skunk

Four species of skunks range into the deserts of North America. The Striped Skunk (Mephitis mephitis) is the largest of the four, reaching fourteen pounds in weight and being about the size of a house cat. The Spotted Skunk (Spilogale putorious) is considerably smaller at a maximum weight of nearly two pounds. It is much less frequently seen and comparatively little known. The Hognose (Conepatus leuconotus) and Hooded Skunks (Mephitis macroura) are both species from Mexico that range into the Chihuahuan and Sonoran Deserts as far west as central Arizona. They are smaller than the Striped Skunk reaching just five pounds in weight.

The striking black and white coloration of all four species is a ready indicator of "skunk," not just to humans but to other predators as well. Unlike most mammals which possess concealing coloration to camouflage themselves, skunks advertise their presence to ward off enemies. It is, of course, their possession of a noxious odor which allows their warning coloration to function. Skunks have two scent glands near the base of their tail. Each one is surrounded by muscle tissue and has a duct leading to a small nozzle. These nozzles can be voluntarily protruded from the anus, aimed at an enemy and, through contractions of the muscles surrounding the scent glands, eject fine yellow droplets up to 25 feet.

The active ingredient in the foul smelling fluid is known as n-butyl mercaptan. It can be perceived by humans if as little as 0.000,000,000,000,07 ounce is inhaled. It has a penetrating odor which causes nausea or even temporary blindness should sufficient quantities come in contact with the eyes. Even the skunk can't stand the odor and vigorously tries to clean itself should any of the liquid catch in its fur.

Skunks only discharge their chemical armament when provoked. They first perform much foot stamping and forward lunges to warn their assailant. Only if these antics don't work do they discharge. Hooded and Striped Skunks turn their tail toward the enemy and make short scoots backward when firing. Spotted Skunks do an amusing handstand looking directly forward and firing the fine spray over their head. All four species are highly accurate.

Skunks emerge at night to feed on beetles, grasshoppers, a variety of rodents, and fruit. Spotted Skunks obtain their food requirements within a home range of somewhat less than 200 acres. Striped Skunks, although much larger, require less feeding territory--usually under twenty acres. This difference partially reflects the moister and more productive habitat of the Striped Skunk.

All species breed in winter with females giving birth to between four and seven young. Striped and Hognose Skunks have a gestation period of two months whereas Spotted Skunk gestation may be twice as long. The long gestation period of the Spotted Skunk is probably a result of "delayed implantation" as is found in many other members of the weasel family as well as some species of bats. In this phenomenon, fertilized eggs become dormant in the blastocyst stage for many weeks. At the end of this period they move to the uterine wall, implant in it and continue on with development. Of course this process lengthens the gestation period but has the advantage of the young being born in May or June, the time when the Spotted Skunk's food is most abundant.

None of our skunks hibernate or estivate although Striped Skunks may become dormant for long periods of inclement weather. Caution should be practiced around wild skunks as they are known to contract rabies.

DESCRIPTION: The black and white markings make skunks unmistakable. The cat-sized torso, full body stripes and white "V" on the back distinguish the Striped Skunk. The Hooded Skunk lacks the white V and has a fifteen-inch tail that is twice the length of the Striped Skunk. The Hognose Skunk has a long piglike snout and white tail. The Spotted Skunk is kitten-sized and has numerous short stripes.

DISTRIBUTION: Both the Striped and Spotted skunks are found throughout the North American deserts, in suitable habitat. The Striped Skunk is, in desert regions, most often associated with agricultural and suburban environments or within one mile of river bottoms or large springs where a permanent supply of water exists. The Spotted Skunk prefers rocky areas and is more tolerant of arid conditions than are the other three species of skunks. The Hognose and Hooded Skunks are restricted to the Chihuahuan and eastern Sonoran Deserts of Arizona, New Mexico and Texas. Hooded and Hognose Skunks are usually found in brushy or rocky areas.

Coyotes are by no means restricted to the North American deserts. In fact, they are probably more common on grasslands and high mesas. Yet so adaptable are these collie-sized canines that nearly every habitat in western North America has its share of Coyotes--and deserts are no exception.

Coyotes (_Canis latrans_) from hot desert regions have several special characteristics that set them apart from their high mountain brethren. Their smaller size is the most notable trait. Desert Coyotes weigh about twenty pounds, less than half the weight of mountain individuals that may reach fifty. It is widely believed this reflects the selective advantage of small size since small animals are able to radiate excess body heat back into the environment more rapidly than larger individuals. The fur of desert Coyotes is also shorter, thinner and more pale. Pale colors tend to absorb less heat than darker ones as well as blend into the light background of most desert habitats.

Contrary to popular belief, Coyotes feed extensively on plant material. In one study conducted in Anza-Borrego Desert State Park, it was found that vegetable matter made up 40% of the Coyotes diet. Such things as grasses, seeds, fruits, and flowers were eaten regularly. Meat, of course, is important and is obtained from carrion, rodents, rabbits and arthropods. Coyotes occasionally hunt in groups of from two to eight individuals, especially if large prey is involved. Young Bighorn Sheep and deer may be attacked in this manner. Even badgers have been known to be killed by Coyotes working together.

Howling is not the most frequent part of Coyote vocalizations regardless of what romantic western movies may suggest. A series of short yips is more typical and is often done in the company of several other Coyotes. This is one way in which Coyotes communicate with each other, revealing their moods and whereabouts.

Males and females often travel together even before they breed in January or February. Both sexes participate in rearing the pups which are born about two months after mating. Mother of course provides milk from her mammary glands. Both parents also regurgitate the contents of their stomachs. From four to seven young comprise the average litter with exceptional cases of twelve being recorded. Within fourteen days the pups have opened their eyes and by six weeks are hunting with their parents. By twelve months of age they are on their own and have staked out their territory marked with the scent of their urine.

Coyotes are relentlessly persecuted for their depredations on livestock and pets. That they are occasionally predators of sheep, calves, and poultry is certain. However, it is equally certain that the intensity with which they (and tens of thousands of other animals that are inadvertantly killed) are slaughtered in the name of livestock protection far exceeds justification. Department of Interior figures show that in a typical year in the 1960s, 85,000 Coyotes were poisoned, shot or trapped. In New Mexico alone in 1975, 5,200 were eliminated by a single governmental agency--the Animal Damage Control. These programs continue today and raise serious questions about the actual harm done to livestock when compared to the cost of extermination programs directed against one of our last large predators.

DESCRIPTION: In deserts, the Coyote are slightly smaller than a collie with gray or tan fur and a bushy tail held low when running.

DISTRIBUTION: Found throughout the North American deserts in most habitats.

Coyote eating jackrabbit carcass - photograph by Hans Baerwald, courtesy Palm Springs Desert Museum

Kit Fox and Gray Fox

The Kit Fox is one of the desert's most appealing creatures. Its four-pound body, slight limbs and soft, pale fur make for a dainty appearance, in contrast to the harsh environment in which it lives.

Unfortunately, few people get to see the Kit Fox, Vulpes macrotis. Like nearly all desert carnivores, it is primarily nocturnal and does not emerge from its burrow until dusk--a time when people move indoors. A Kit Fox also prefers wide open flats and avoids the canyons and other sheltered areas where campers frequent. It's no wonder that those who are lucky enough to glimpse one of these big-eared mammals will not likely forget the encounter.

The vast majority of my sightings have occurred at night when foxes dash in front of my automobile head-light beams. Fortunately I have been able to avoid a collision, yet the many roadside carcasses I have seen are a grizzly testimonial to the significance of this kind of mortality on Kit Fox populations. Rarely do I see a fox abroad during daylight hours. My first daytime sighting occurred while driving slowly along a little-used road in Anza-Borrego Desert State Park. The fox was about 75 yards off and trotting straight across a flat toward some low mounds when it disappeared. I got out and walked to the site where the fox vanished and found a burrow with an entrance about ten inches high. Not more than six feet away was another opening, obviously a second entrance and as well-used as the first.

I set up camp some fifty yards from the burrow entrance. I wanted to get some photographs of the fox and so at dusk placed some meat scraps and a can of water on the ground near my sleeping bag to attract it. I did not wait long. As the sky turned from blue to black and a dozen or so stars came into view, the fox appeared just beyond the bait. Though shy, it methodically approached and sampled the food. Not surprisingly my camera flash startled it, but within ten minutes it was back eating.

It returned at ten that evening, again at two and for the last time at four-thirty that morning. It ate all the meat but did not drink the water. This was surprising since surface water was no where to be found and perennial vegetation was scant with no spring annuals to suggest even a moderately wet winter. Since the month was April, the Sonoran Desert was warm enough that a fox would drink if it needed to. But I had to remind myself that Kit Foxes are carnivores whose food is mostly water. As long as the fox had enough to eat and conserved water at every opportunity, drinking water was not necessary. My nocturnal visitor appeared well nourished and was obviously doing quite nicely on its diet of kangaroo rats and jackrabbits.

Kit Foxes show surprising versatility in their choice of prey. In the Great Basin Desert of Utah they tackle four--pound jackrabbits which account for 94% of their food intake. (These must be tremendous battles since a jackrabbit is the same size as a Kit Fox.) By comparison, kangaroo rats are their dietary mainstay in portions of arid California. Many other foods are eaten including ground squirrels, pocket mice, lizards, scorpions, an occasional bird, and a variety of plant material. Occasionally, smaller animals may be buried near the burrow and eaten later. A Kit Fox rarely travels more than a mile in search of food. It may travel with its mate on forays but there is no coordinated strategy as sometimes observed in Coyotes.

It is no coincidence that the Kit Fox is the smallest canine in North America. Small animals are able to rid themselves of excess body heat more readily than large ones, just like a cup of hot coffee cools faster than a full pot. In a desert environment this is a distinct advantage for a nocturnal animal that is active on warm nights. Of course a small animal is at a disadvantage in winter when conserving, rather than losing, heat is of the utmost importance. Naturalists have yet to answer this qaundry of competing needs at different seasons, but perhaps Kit Foxes are more often abroad during daylight hours in winter and switch to a strictly nocturnal existence during the warm months.

It is likely that a second environmental factor also selects for small size. Because of the desert's aridity and resultant low productivity, food is not as plentiful as in wetter environments. A small animal should be at an advantage in an arid environment since it is less difficult for it to find sufficient food. In captivity, a four-pound Kit Fox eats about one pound of food per day. The Gray Fox, Urocyon cinereoargenteus, weighs nearly twice as much and requires over two pounds of food per day. As one might expect, the Gray Fox is found in less arid and more productive habitats than is the Kit Fox.

The large ears of the Kit Fox are distinctive. They are filled with coarse hairs that help exclude sand and, relative to body size, are twice as large as those of the Gray Fox. It is likely they play some role in sharpening hearing acuity, an important adaptation in a nocturnal hunter, but their importance in getting rid of excess heat should not be under-

Kit Fox - photograph by Robert L. Leatherman

stated. Just as a car radiatior functions to cool off hot water by convection, the large ears of the Kit Fox are filled with tiny capillaries that bring warm blood close to cool night air. So long as the air is a few degrees cooler than the blood, heat will be lost to the atmosphere. Several other desert animals possess long ears including the jackrabbit and burro and all are considered examples of Allen's Rule which asserts that mammals from hot climates have longer extremities than those from cold environments.

A Kit Fox often lives and hunts in areas of loose, wind-blown sand. Its feet have dense hairs which increase the amount of foot contact with the sand and thus improve traction and make for more efficient digging. These hairs are so dense that kit fox tracks rarely show the claw or pad marks that are typical of other canines.

Breeding begins in late fall or early winter with the female usually giving birth to four young in February or March. The exact gestation period is unknown but it is assumed to approximate that of the Gray Fox which is about 51 days. Both parents feed the pups; the mother with her milk and the father who captures them small rodents. The entire family may occupy a den or the male may have his own burrow nearby. By late summer the family separates and the pups disperse.

This is a critical time in the life of a young Kit Fox for it must move through unknown territory and is highly vulnerable to predators. It also must find food entirely on its own. Unlike most carnivores, the Kit Fox shares hunting ranges with other members of its species. A pup that survives through its first year does not breed until its second year and probably lives five or six years. Premature death is most often a result of an illegal shooting or automobile collison. Some Kit Foxes are eaten by other predators such as Bobcats, Coyotes or Golden Eagles.

DESCRIPTION: Small size (about the size of a house cat), large ears, black-tipped tail, and pale color distinguish the Kit Fox from the Gray Fox, the only other fox living within its range.

DISTRIBUTION: Found throughout the North American deserts on flat, open terrain. Though rarely seen, it can be the most abundant carnivore within its habitat. In many regions Kit Foxes have been eliminated because of destruction of their habitat by humans. The Gray Fox is also widespread but prefers areas where rocks or brush provide cover.

Known by several names including Wildcat, Desert Lynx and Bobcat, this twenty-pound-desert dweller is seldom seen by even the most keen-eyed observer. Nocturnal habits, avoidance of humans, preference for brushy areas, and small numbers as a result of its position on top of the food chain account for its apparent rarity. Strangely, most of my personal observations have been of Bobcats resting on the tops of utility poles. In rural desert areas, residents often allow their pet dogs to run free and two or more can "tree" a Bobcat. The cat often remains on the pole until the following evening when darkness hides its escape.

Unlike foxes and Coyotes, Bobcats (Lynx rufus) are essentially carnivorous. Cottontails, jackrabbits, ground squirrels, mice, pocket gophers, woodrats and quail are favored prey with an occasional snake or lizard added to the menu when available. There are a few records of young deer being captured. Whatever the prey, its presence is detected by sight and/or sound, not by scent as is often true for canids. Again in contrast to canids, Bobcats utilize an ambush or surprise attack to capture prey as their musculature is structured for quickness and power rather than endurance.

Although breeding can occur at any time of year, the young most often are born in April or May after a sixty-day gestation period. Two kittens, blind at birth and weighing from four to eight ounces, comprise a normal-sized litter though litters of four are not unusual. The kittens' eyes open in ten days and it will be nine or ten months before they leave their mother. She prepares them for hunting on their own by bringing live food home and by encouraging them to follow her by keeping their eyes on her white-tipped tail as they travel through the brush. The father plays no role whatsoever in the rearing of the kittens.

The young are born in a deep rock crevice or burrow, the types of shelters also used by solitary adult Bobcats. It is thought that Bobcats do not dig their own burrow but rather usurp one from some other animal. Bobcats are solitary animals with males and females spending only a few days together during courtship and mating. Males are fertile by the end of their first year whereas females usually do not give birth to their first litter until they are two years of age. Females normally produce one litter per year.

It is an unfortunate reality that such a beautiful and interesting predator is still hunted for sport and fur. Although an occasional lamb, chicken or young pig may be taken by these felines, their raids on domestic animals are so rare that no justification for predator control exists. The increasing rarity and near extinction of many species of wild spotted cats and the lack of protection for Bobcats has initiated a new drive for Bobcat pelts shoving prices up from $20 per pelt in 1970 to as high as $150 in 1985. Some fear the Bobcat may be precariously close to extinction before this enterprise is banned.

The size of the territory roamed by an individual cat varies tremendously. On average most females stay within an area about two miles in diameter though movements up to 25 miles and return are known. The lifespan of a free-ranging Bobcat is about ten years. Captive individuals have been known to reach an age of 25 years.

DESCRIPTION: Twenty- to thirty-pound weight, spotted fur, flared facial ruff, and short stubby tail distinguish this desert cat from all other animals within its range. Unlike domestic cats, Bobcats have oval rather than vertical pupils.

DISTRIBUTION: To be expected in all habitats but reaches greatest densities, one per square mile, in rocky and brushy areas. Ranges throughout the North American Desert.

Bobcat - photograph by Norm Wakeman

Ground Squirrels

The desert environment can place rigorous demands upon its inhabitants. Intense aridity, scorching daytime temperatures and intermittent food shortages are just some of the conditions that must be dealt with. However, North American desert animals have coped with these problems for thousands, in some cases millions, of years, ample time to evolve a number of impressive adaptations for survival.

Ground squirrels are a case in a point. At least twelve different species range into our North American deserts and most of them have the amazing ability to turn down their metabolic thermostat and go without food or water for months. Physiological signals cause them to enter their burrows and gradually go into a state of "torpor." Their body temperature drops at least twenty degrees--to a point one to three degrees above burrow air temperature--and their breathing rate slows to just one breath every three minutes or even less. They are quite immobile during this period: in what appears to be a deep sleep. The torpor is not continuous, however. Every few days or weeks there is a brief rewarming and arousal (but not necessarily an appearance above ground) for up to two days, before the next cooling and torpor. The large amount of fat that squirrels accumulate prior to entering torpor (up to 30% of their body weight) is required for the rewarming process that occurs intermittently throughout the entire dormant period.

Humans, of course, cannot tolerate such a drop in body temperature. A decrease of only a few degrees quickly causes an array of bodily processes to malfunction which can result in death. Just how the squirrels survive is not fully understood at this time. Somehow, through appropriate biochemical reactions, they maintain the integrity of their tissues and sustain minimal metabolic activity.

The advantages to the ground squirrels are tremendous. With a lowered metabolic rate, less energy in the form of food or fat is required, and less water for bodily processes is needed. In fact, these needs are so reduced that adult Round-tailed Ground Squirrels (Spermophilus tereticaudus) are known to remain inactive for up to six months per year. Periods of torpor coincide with unfavorable periods of the year such as winter and summer when food or moisture may be scarce. Most ground squirrels hibernate in winter--others (the Round-tailed Ground Squirrel and its close relative, the Mojave Ground Squirrel, Spermophilus mohavensis) may also estivate during all or part of the summer. Both of these seasons can be difficult because of food shortages and the summer months can be exceptionally dry in certain desert re-

Round-tailed Ground Squirrel - photograph by Hans Baerwald, courtesy Palm Springs Desert Museum

gions.

However, not all ground squirrels enter torpor. The Whitetail Antelope, Yuma Antelope, and Texas Antelope Squirrels do not estivate or hibernate. All three species are active year round, even during the hot summer months. By allowing their body temperatures to rise with the daytime temperature (up to 108° F), continually running into their cool burrows to unload excess heat, and feeding on moist food whenever possible they are able to maintain a favorable water balance.

Most desert ground squirrels cache food for emergencies although not to the extent of tree squirrels and chipmunks. Seeds and greens are stuffed into expandable cheek pouches located inside their mouths, then carried to hiding places either above or below ground. Only dry food is stored; greens, insects, and occasional nestling birds or eggs are consumed on the spot.

Ground squirrels are known to occasionally be reservoirs for the bacterium, Pasteurella pestis. When present in the blood of humans, it results in plague or "bubonic plague" as it is more widely known. The disease can be fatal to humans, squirrels, and even the fleas which transmit it.

Fleas sit about the entrance of ground squirrel tunnels waiting for an opportunity to attach to the occupant. Once attached, blood is sucked up by the flea and, if the squirrel is a carrier, the bacterium is also ingested. Infected fleas may then find their way to humans and infect them during feeding. Either the flea disgorges into the wound made by the proboscis, or defecates while feeding and the material is rubbed into the opening by the victim responding to the irritation of the puncture.

Most ground squirrels do not harbor the plague bacterium, and when they do rarely is there an opportunity for the flea to infect a human. Potentially high risk areas are campgrounds where ground squirrels abound. During early summer, ground squirrel numbers reach their peak as a result of spring litters and it is at this time that chances of contact are greatest. Cases of plague are exceedingly rare. The dusting of rodent holes with flea powder and the strategic closing of certain campsites by health department officials is largely responsible for the scarcity of infections.

In general, female ground squirrels mate within five days

after initiating spring activity. From three to nine young are born within about 28 days after fertilization. The male plays no role in the rearing of the young.

DESCRIPTION: Ground dwelling, diurnal habits and lack of stripes on the face distinguish ground squirrels from all other desert rodents. These are the only small desert mammals that are active during the day in summer and late spring. Some species may reach thirteen inches in length excluding the tail.

DISTRIBUTION: Found throughout the North American deserts in most habitats.

Antelope Ground Squirrel - photograph by Hans Baerwald, courtesy Palm Springs Desert Museum

These two groups are members of a mammalian family known as Heteromyidae, and as such possess a number of u- nique characteristics not found among other North American desert rodents. Most noticeable are the large and powerful hind legs and the small front legs, reminiscent of Australian kangaroos. This feature enables kangaroo rats (genus Dipodo- mys), to have an effective "saltatorial" or hopping mode of locomotion when moving rapidly. Instantaneous right angle turns and a bobbing forward movement are both advantages of this style of locomotion, making kangaroo rats difficult for predators to catch. In an open, treeless desert habitat where hiding places are few and prey animals are exposed, such an adaptation is at a premium. Saltation is also consid- ered to be highly efficient when food resources are widely scattered as they are in deserts. It takes less energy for a kangaroo rat to move one hundred feet to a seed pile than it does for a quadruped of the same body weight.

The relatively large heads of kangaroo rats and pocket mice are a second distinctive anatomical feature and are a result of the huge auditory bullae which surround the middle ears and function to intensify sounds. These enable Hetero- myids to hear predators early and maximize their chances of escaping.

Located on either side of their mouths are external fur- -lined pockets in which food is carried back to the burrows. There is no opening between these pockets and the mouth and the contents must be removed before they can be eaten. The front feet are inserted far back into these pockets and the contents are scooped out and stored, or consumed on the spot.

Both kangaroo rats and pocket mice can survive without access to drinking water, and do not even require succulent food. They obtain their water from seeds, which appear dry but contain up to 10% water, and from the metabolism of food which produces water as a by-product. Of course other animal groups obtain water through these means. What makes Heteromyids so interesting is that they can survive without any additional sources of moisture. This is because they are extremely efficient at conserving what moisture they do obtain. Their nocturnal existence and burrowing habits and resultant reduction in evaporative water loss from lung and skin surfaces are certainly the most important con- servation measures. But they also possess several physiologi- cal mechanisms as well. The kidneys of Heteromyids are highly efficient at eliminating excess salts and protein waste products without the use of large amounts of water. Both

Kangaroo Rat - photograph by Hans Baerwald, courtesy Palm Springs Desert Museum

Pocket Mouse

kangaroo rats and pocket mice can produce a urine five times more concentrated than that of humans and thus save appreciable amounts of water during urination. Water is also conserved by producing feces that have 50% less water than those of humans. Lastly, moist expired air from the lungs is cooled as it passes through the nasal passageways. This occurs because the passageways are cooler than the air due to evaporation from their surfaces during inhalation. As warm, moist air from the lungs passes over these surfaces, some water condenses on the nasal walls before it passes out. Much of this water is reabsorbed when the animal inhales.

Breeding usually begins in late winter providing late fall and winter rains are at or above average. Below average precipitation during this season often results in a decrease or, if the drought is severe, a cessation of breeding activity. In favorable years the numbers of pocket mice and kangaroo rats may increase ten-fold. From one to four young comprise a litter and up to four litters are produced each year.

DESCRIPTION: Large heads, small ears and fur-lined cheek pouches distinguish kangaroo rats and pocket mice from other rodent groups. Fourteen species of pocket mice (Genus Perognathus) occupy the North American deserts. All have a head and body length under five inches and lack distinctive facial markings. Six species of kangaroo rats exist in the deserts of North America. They are generally larger than pocket mice and some have a head and body length up to 6 1/2 inches. Kangaroo rats have proportionately larger hind legs and distinctive white facial markings.

DISTRIBUTION: As a group, kangaroo rats tend to be found in open desert scrub habitat and usually avoid rocky areas. In contrast, pocket mice are found in open, brushy or rocky habitats. At least one pocket mouse and kangaroo rat species is found in each of the North American deserts.

White-footed Mouse

These are some of our most abundant mammals. Their numbers are known to reach twenty per acre and are found in every habitat, from below sea level to over 9,000 feet in the highest mountains.

Eight species of white-footed mice occur within the boundaries of the North American Desert and at least one species is found in each of five desert subdivisions. Their success is due to their utilization of a variety of both plant and animal foods, their ability to climb up shrubs and slick rock surfaces, their capacity to evade harsh conditions, and their high reproductive rate. Breeding activity is most intense in spring and fall and females may give birth to four litters per year with up to eight young per litter. This is the highest reproductive rate of any desert mammal.

Although many white-footed mice nest in burrows, several species do not hesitate in building their nests beneath surface litter or in dense shrubs and trees. I have even seen them scamper up the naked trunks of sixty-foot Desert Fan Palms to their nests. This seems at odds with the habits of most rodents which remain below ground during the hot daylight hours. I suspect that such individuals have access to moist food to compensate for the moisture they must lose by exposure to relatively hot midday temperatures. In addition, above ground nesting may be restricted to spring and fall when temperatures are mild. At other times these mice probably seek refuge in the abandoned burrows of other rodents. At least one member of the group, the Cactus Mouse, Peromyscus eremicus, has evolved the capacity to lower its metabolic rate and become torpid when food or water is in short supply. In such a state it lies dormant through much of the hot summer. The Canyon Mouse, P. crinitus, is the only white-footed mouse species that can survive on a diet of dry seeds (in laboratory tests) and concentrate waste products in its urine to a degree comparable to kangaroo rats.

Should a white-footed mouse ever find its way into your desert home or campsite, it's not likely to go unnoticed. As a nocturnal rodent, it scampers around in the otherwise quiet of the night--chewing, scratching, and climbing into every conceivable niche. The resulting sounds can be a bit disconcerting and some persons no doubt would swear that prowlers are near. The following morning usually reveals what manner of creature was about. Holes in food packages, bits of refuse stuffed in corners, and tiny black droppings are all evidence that a white-footed mouse, not a prowler, was present.

Occasionally my own family unwillingly spends the night with these shy, one-ounce creatures. Like most dwellings, our home has an outside entrance just large enough for mice but too small for us to find. Fortunately they can be easily captured and we are usually able to evict them in a few days.

DESCRIPTION: Long tails, white feet, large ears and bodies less than four inches in length distinguish members of the genus _Peromyscus_ from most other desert rodents. White-footed mice are distinguished from pocket mice by their lack of external cheek pouches.

DISTRIBUTION: At least one of the eight species of white-footed mice can be expected at most locations in the North American deserts. Reaches greatest abundance where shrubs or trees are dense or in the vicinity of rock outcrops.

Palm oasis in Anza-Borrego Desert State Park

Other than ground squirrels, these are the only desert rodents you might encounter during the day. In winter and early spring, woodrats are occasionally seen running through brush or beneath rock piles. More often they are observed at dusk poking their heads out from their nests just before embarking upon a nocturnal search for food and nest material.

The woodrat is sometimes referred to as a "trading rat" because of its habit of picking up an object and leaving another in its place. These items are carried to its nest and deposited on or around the large, above ground pile of debris which functions as its house. Nest structures may reach four feet in height and resemble a pile of junk consisting mostly of sticks and cactus joints. Since the woodrat often lives in close proximity to homes and campsites, construction material may include watches, coins, tin cans, with even an upper denture plate being recorded as nest-building material. The "trading" propensity results from the woodrat's inability to carry more than one object in its mouth at a time. It drops one, picks up another, and moves on.

The woodrat house has two main functions: it provides insulation against temperature extremes and protection from predators. Since many woodrat nests are situated at, or even slightly above ground level, it might seem that the rodent would be subjected to dangerously high temperatures during the summer months. However, most nests are built beneath rocks or large shrubs which protect the nest from direct sunlight. In addition, the huge pile of debris acts as a thermal blanket, retarding the flow of hot air into the center of the nest during the summer and reducing the outward flow of the woodrat's own body heat during the winter. Even on hot summer days when soil temperatures may rise to 167° F, the soil beneath the nest does not exceed 115° F and the nest interior seldom exceeds 88° F. In extremely hot portions of the Southwest, a woodrat may build its nest slightly below ground level or beneath a deep rock pile. The woodrat house also affords some protection from enemies. Cholla joints, pieces of glass, and sharp metal objects can deter many predators. In fact the only animal that makes a habit of tearing woodrat nests apart is the Badger. A woodrat is most vulnerable when it is foraging away from its nest. At such times it may become prey for a Coyote, fox, snake or owl.

Woodrat nests are seldom vacant. If the occupant dies, another woodrat soon moves in and begins adding more debris to the pile. Some nests are known to be over ten thousand years old and have equally old plant remains buried in their centers. These remains may be so well preserved that their age and identity can be determined. Pieces of ancient pine trees have been taken from woodrat nests even though pines may no longer occur in the vicinity of the nest. From this and other evidence, scientists have determined that the North American deserts were probably cooler and received more rainfall in the past than they do today.

The food of woodrats must be succulent since their water conserving abilities are not nearly as refined as those of pocket mice and kangaroo rats. Cactus or yuccas are especially important and woodrats may not be able to occupy an area if these plants are not available. Flowers, seeds, fruits, insects and carrion are also eaten.

Two drawbacks of relying upon cactus for moisture are the sharp spines and the high concentrations of oxalic acid. Woodrats are the only rodents that are sufficiently nimble to reach the succulent tissue without regularly being stabbed. With remarkable care they orient the segments so that the least number of spines are pointed in their direction, bite off any misaligned spines, and push their mouth to the juicy cactus. Once they have chewed an opening they confine their feeding to the margins of the original bite and simply continue to enlarge it. Should they become impaled, they do not panic, as do many other rodents, but remain calm and bite off the offending spines at the surface of their skin. The oxalic acid in cactus can also cause problems for mammals. It combines with calcium in the digestive tract to form calcium oxalate crystals. These crystals cannot normally be absorbed into a mammal's system and ultimately can result in a calcium deficiency. The crystals can also damage the kidneys and even lead to death. The woodrat's system renders these calcium oxalate crystals harmless, though the mechanism by which it does this is unknown.

Female woodrats have been known to deliver as many as five litters per year with up to five young per litter. The young open their eyes at twelve days and are weaned at from sixteen to forty-two days depending upon the health of the mother and the size of the litter. They become sexually mature at sixty days. Lactation demands may be so great on the mother that she dies after weaning. Curiously, if young woodrats are nursing when disturbed by an intruder, the mother will scamper off to safety with the young attached to her nipples.

DESCRIPTION: Five species of woodrats are found in the

North American deserts. In general, they are characterized by their six-inch bodies, large ears, white bellies and gray to brown fur.

DISTRIBUTION: At least one of the five species of wood-rats found in the North American Desert exists in any given region. Found from below sea level to the top of desert mountain ranges. Absent from areas of loose, windblown sand. Most common in rocky areas where cactus is abundant.

Woodrat - photograph by Hans Baerwald, courtesy Palm Springs Desert Museum

Desert Cottontail - photograph by Robert L. Leatherman

This is one of our most abundant and best known desert mammals. Its tremendous reproductive rate, darting escape manuevers, and willingness to feed upon a wide variety of plants are the major factors in its success.

Unlike its jackrabbit cousin, the Desert Cottontail is a true rabbit, not a hare, and is born without fur, with eyes closed, and inability to move about for the first ten days. The mother also makes a fur-lined nest, again in contrast with the jackrabbit. The nest may be constructed in the open, but in desert areas it is usually formed underground in a borrowed hole or in one excavated by the female.

From one to five young make up an average-sized litter. Birth occurs from 26 to 30 days after mating and the young are weaned in two weeks. By human standards, cottontail mothers are not very attentive, often nursing their young just once a day. With a year-round breeding season in years of above average precipitation, a single female can produce six litters annually for a total of up to thirty offspring. These offspring can reach sexual maturity in as few as eighty days.

A high rate of reproduction is a necessity for an animal that is prey for many carnivores. Although the cottontail can run up to twenty miles per hour and follow a zigzag pattern that is the envy of any downhill skier, it is frequently captured before it reaches the safety of the dense rocks or vegetation that it requires for protection. Coyotes, foxes, Bobcats, stray dogs, owls and even Gopher Snakes are just a few of the more common predators, and so it is not surprising that the average cottontail is able to escape its enemies for just two years.

Cottontails usually spend the hours of darkness feeding, although in winter they may remain active through the morning. An acre of suitable habitat is likely to harbor from one to four individuals, any one of which may move over a twenty acre home range in search of food. (Under ideal conditions of abundant food and cover, numbers may reach fifteen individuals per acre.) Grasses, leaves, acorns and other fruit, and many forbs are regularly eaten and during times of severe drought even cactus may be included in their diet.

Both cottontails and jackrabbits are known to carry two communicable diseases which have resulted in human deaths. Tularemia is caused by a bacteria known as Francisella tularensis and is usually contracted by a human while handling a sick or recently killed rabbit. Infected ticks or other arthropods attach themselves to the skin and introduce the pathogen when they feed. Although the vast majority of victims survive, most must endure pain and fever for up to six weeks with a lengthy convalescence. Relapsing Fever is also carried primarily by rabbits and it, too, is caused by the introduction of a bacterial organism into the body. Ticks and lice are the mechanisms of transfer from rabbits to humans and thus infection usually occurs from direct contact. The disease in man is characterized by an acute onset of fever three to ten days after infection. Penicillin and tetracyclines are effective in treatment. Although few people actually contract these diseases, it is wise to avoid direct contact with wild rabbits.

DESCRIPTION: Although four species of cottontails are found in the North American deserts, it is the Desert Cottontail, _Sylvilagus_ _auduboni_, that is the most abundant and widespread. The Desert Cottontail has lighter-colored fur and longer ears than the other three species, characteristics that help it dissipate heat. The cottony white tail, short legs and relatively short ears distinguish the Desert Cottontail from jackrabbits. Head and body length is about fourteen inches and large individuals may weigh as much as four pounds.

DISTRIBUTION: Cottontails are usually absent from open flats where jackrabbits are superior competitors. Cluttered habitats with large boulders and dense shrubs to provide shelter from both predators and climatic extremes most likely to provide suitable homes. The Desert Cottontail is found within all five of the North American deserts.

These animals require little introduction. As our most conspicuous desert mammal, they are predictable in their occurrence and are recognized on sight by most desert visitors. High densities (up to two per acre), huge ears and non-burrowing habits are the primary reasons for their familiarity.

For many years biologists have been fascinated with desert jackrabbits because of their ability to maintain large and widespread populations without relying upon burrows, drinking water, or carnivorism to maintain water balance. Under natural conditions, jackrabbits are not known to burrow. They scratch out small depressions under shrubs for shelter and spend the hot, daylight hours resting in these "forms." Unlike their relatives, the cottontails, they miss out on the cool temperatures and high humidities of an underground shelter and thus must evaporate water from their respiratory surfaces to keep cool on hot days.

This would not seem a problem so long as drinking water was available to replace that which is lost through evaporative cooling. Bighorn Sheep and Burros use this strategy and, in fact, jackrabbits are frequently observed drinking at waterholes. The paradox is that the vast majority of jacks do not have access to drinking water and, since they are herbivores, do not eat the moist tissues of other animals as do predators such as Coyotes and Bobcats. Obviously they must either reduce their evaporative water loss or utilize some other food that has a high water content.

Part of the solution does involve the jackrabbit's diet. Cactus is eaten at times and mesquite leaves are readily consumed as are leaves of many succulent desert plants. These contain significantly more water than the grain which makes up the diet of kangaroo rats and pocket mice but often less than the animal food of a carnivore. Thus a leafy diet helps, but jackrabbits must still utilize water conserving techniques to compensate for a lifestyle that might otherwise leave them with a water deficit.

Reductions in the amount of water lost through evaporation certainly can conserve water but might seem difficult for an animal that exists on the desert's surface. However, jackrabbits are very good at keeping cool without necessarily resorting to the use of evaporative cooling by panting. (Jackrabbits do not sweat.) They feed at night, remain in the shade during the day, and avoid physical activity when possible. Other adaptive behaviors are far more subtle. The form which they dig is slightly below ground level and thus is cooler than the surface soil. There is some evidence that they may even dig very shallow burrows during conditions of intense heat. In either a form or a burrow their body comes in contact with cool soil and excess heat is transferred via conduction to the ground. When on the surface they may orient themselves to the northern sky (with erect ears that account for 20% of their body surface) and radiate any excess heat into the atmosphere. Combined, these adjustments reduce the jackrabbit's potential evaporative water loss up to 70% and enable it to survive on the moisture it receives from its food. Additional water is conserved by producing relatively dry feces that are drier and a urine that is more concentrated than those excreted by domestic rabbits.

Breeding occurs through much of the year with up to seven young per litter and up to fourteen offspring per year. The young jacks are born with their eyes open and fully furred, unlike cottontails that are born blind and naked. No nest is constructed and newborn jacks are simply born under a shrub. Apparently the mother only returns to nurse her young. Within three to four weeks they are weaned and can approach the forty-miles-per-hour top speed of the adults.

Curiously, jackrabbits eat some of their own fecal material. Two kinds of fecal pellets are formed--hard, normal droppings produced in the intestine and soft pellets formed in the cecum. The latter kind are composed mainly of bacteria and are taken directly from the anus and consumed. This process of running some food through the digestive system twice aids in releasing important nutrients and vitamins locked up in the plants consumed by jackrabbits.

DESCRIPTION: Huge ears, long legs and 17- to 21-inch length distinguish jackrabbits from cottontails, the only other mammal with which they are likely to be confused. (Jackrabbits are not true rabbits but are referred to as hares. They differ from rabbits in that the young are born fully furred and with their eyes open.) The Blacktail Jackrabbit, Lepus californicus, averages only about five pounds, considerably less than the 7 1/2-pound Antelope Jackrabbit, L. alleni. In addition to its larger size, the latter species is also distinguished by its whitish sides and absence of black on its ears.

DISTRIBUTION: Blacktail Jackrabbits are found throughout each of the North American deserts, from below sea level to 12,000 feet. Antelope Jackrabbits are restricted to the Sonoran Desert of central Arizona and adjacent Sonora, Mexico. Both prefer open desert or low hills.

Black-tailed Jackrabbit - photograph by Hans Baerwald, courtesy
Palm Springs Desert Museum

Peccary

Peccaries are often referred to as wild pigs, yet they are no more related to pigs than are hippopotamuses. The similarities in appearance are superficial and reflect similar habits rather than common evolutionary histories. Both are even-toed hoofed mammals and belong to the order Artiodactyla but belong to different mammalian families, Suidae or true pigs and Tayassuidae or peccaries. Some of the most notable differences include the numbers of toes on the hind foot (three in Collared Peccaries, four in pigs), the possession of a complex stomach (a condition not found in pigs), and the presence of a scent gland on the back among peccaries.

Peccaries have a formidable appearance when cornered. The bristles that comprise the "collar" run from the top of the shoulder down both sides and are erected when the peccary is alarmed. This makes the animal look bigger and, when combined with the bearing of the 1 1/2-inch canine teeth, an appearance of ferocity is assured.

However, ferocious does not really describe the behavior of these animals insofar as humans are concerned. The stories that abound with respect to the aggressiveness of Collared Peccaries (Tayassu tajacu) and their attacks on humans are unsubstantiated. I have been unable to find a single record of a human killed or even injured by a wild peccary in the U.S. These tales have no doubt evolved from the peccary's relatively large size (up to 55 pounds), sharp canine teeth that can inflict severe wounds on the only predator of adult peccaries (the Mountain Lion), group defensive behavior, and observations by hunters of wounded animals. In reality, peccaries flee when they detect human presence and should be considered dangerous only if cornered.

As a herbivore, the peccary relies on plant material for food. The pads of prickly pear make up over half its diet. Not infrequently an attempt is made to avoid the long spines by knocking pads to the ground and holding them down with one foot. The skin is then peeled back and the soft flesh eaten from one side. Its caution may be so great that some observers have described peccary feeding behavior as "dainty." The abundance of this cactus species and high water content make prickly pear an attractive staple through most of the year. Indeed, it may be the only reliable food resource in June and early July prior to the onset of summer rains.

Peccaries rarely eat animal foods. In fact, there is no evidence that populations north of the Mexican border eat anything other than roots, tubers, fruits or greens. Only from Mexico and down into South America are they reported to occasionally eat insects, small rodents and bird eggs. Contrary to popular belief, they do not consume rattlesnakes but in fact avoid them.

As an essentially tropical animal, the Collared Peccary is only able to enter portions of the relatively lush Sonoran and Chihuahuan Deserts and then only because of some important behavioral adjustments. Unlike Coyotes and Bobcats, peccaries cannot evaporate sufficient moisture through panting to keep from overheating when exposed to the summer sun. Consequently, they remain in the shade during the day and forage at night during June, July and August. They also remain near permanent sources of drinking water until the arrival of the summer rains when temporary waterholes and moist foods become available. During the winter months, peccaries compensate for the poor insulative qualities of their fur by seeking the shelter of rock overhangs or dense shrubbery and by huddling close together at night. They also bask in the sun on winter days.

Collared Peccaries travel in herds of up to fifty animals though nine individuals per herd is average. Breeding occurs throughout the year. Females usually give birth to two young after a 145-day gestation period. The young mature in about one year and may live to be fifteen years old.

DESCRIPTION: Twenty-four inch height, piglike snout and black and gray fur distinguish this even-toed ungulate.

DISTRIBUTION: Found through most of the Sonoran Desert of Arizona and the Chihuahuan Desert of western Texas. Insufficient rainfall and resultant lack of food and cover prohibit their entry into the California deserts. Cold temperatures inhibit their invasion of the Painted and Great Basin Desert. Brushy areas with abundant cacti are their preferred habitat.

Few animals have been as surrounded by controversy as has the Wild Burro. The species is adored by many people yet has been shot by wildlife biologists intent on restoring the natural order of desert environments.

The Wild Burro (Equus asinus) which thrives in our North American deserts today, was first introduced by the Spaniards in the 1500s. Originally from Africa, these pack animals were prized for their hardiness in arid country. They were sure footed, could locate food in almost barren terrain, and were able to carry heavy burdens through miles of hot, arid country.

Perhaps most impressive is the burro's ability to tolerate a water loss equal to 30% of its body weight (a human requires medical assistance to recover from a 10% weight loss from dehydration). In addition, a burro can replenish the water lost through sweating, urination and defecation after just five minutes of drinking at a waterhole--even after a 25% weight loss due to dehydration. (By contrast, humans require several hours of intermittent drinking to restore even a 5% weight loss.)

It is not surprising that early prospectors relied heavily upon burros as they trekked long distances across the desert in search of gold and silver. But the burros often survived when their owners perished, and many burros escaped or were released to thrive in the environments of the North American deserts. Their numbers have increased to perhaps 18,000 in recent years and there is great concern as to the burros' impact on the desert and its native fauna.

Averaging 350 pounds, adult burros can live nearly 25 years in the wild. During this time productive females may give birth to one colt each year. Since there are no serious diseases or predators, the chances are good that young burros will reach maturity.

Burros feed on a wide variety of plant material. They prefer grasses such as Indian rice grass but many other plants are fed upon including desert tea, palo verde and plantain. Some moisture is obtained through green plant parts but these ungulates must have drinking water throughout the year.

Many naturalists blame Wild Burros for the reduction of certain native animal populations, especially Bighorn Sheep. Competition for water, limited food resources, and habitat destruction are the reasons given for the decline of native wildlife. Furthermore, burro numbers are not controlled through predation, disease, or competition from other ungulates as they are in North Africa. This gives burros an advantage over native fauna. Allowed to run unchecked, burro numbers soon increase to ecologically disastrous levels and can lead to starvation for the burros themselves. At best, the result may be a wholesale reduction of many native plants and animals and, at worst, the extinction of some. Population declines have already been noted for certain native species.

Burros can often be seen during daylight hours in fall, winter and spring. The hot months of summer often result in their foraging at night and in the early morning hours.

DESCRIPTION: Burros stand about 4 1/2 feet at the shoulders with long ears and a short mane running down the back of the neck. Color varies from almost black to creamy or bluish gray.

DISTRIBUTION: Can occur in most habitats. Found throughout much of the North American deserts so long as drinking water is within ten miles.

Mother burro and young

Deer are among the last large mammals found in the North American deserts. Unlike Pronghorn, Wolves and Bighorn Sheep that either have vanished or survive with markedly reduced populations, deer may be more abundant now than they were during the early part of this century. The establishment of artificial waterholes, habitat preservation as is found in state and national parks, the deer's own physical capabilities which allow them to leap over fences and overcome other barriers to dispersal, and the elimination of some natural predators are thought to be responsible for the increase. Deer are also behaviorally flexible as indicated by their change from a dawn and dusk activity pattern to a nocturnal existence in areas frequented by hunters.

Two deer species occupy the North American deserts: the large-eared Mule Deer (Odocoileus hemionus) and the White-tailed Deer (O. virginianus). In the Southwest, Mule Deer are the slightly larger of the two species with bucks reaching 3 1/2 feet at the shoulder and attaining maximum weights of up to 350 pounds. For both species, bucks average 200 and does about 125 pounds. White-tailed Deer can be distinguished from Mule Deer by their manner of flight: Whitetails run with a bobbing gallop, whereas Mule Deer bound away in stiff-legged jumps. Male White-tailed Deer also possess antlers with points branching from the main beam. Mule deer antlers typically branch to form two equal forks. A final distinguishing feature is the tail which is relatively small in mule deer and is black or black-tipped on top. White-tailed deer possess a brownish tail and hold it conspicuously erect when running and thus reveal the white underside.

Only bucks normally grow antlers; bony structures that are cast (dropped) and regrown each year. Antlers are rarely used for defense from predators. The size of the male's antlers are influenced by age, nutrition and genetic factors, and signify social status in relation to other males. The antlers serve to intimidate rivals and are used in head-on clashes. Large-antlered bucks mate most often, and move from group to group in their quest for females in estrous.

Does give birth to one or two fawns in early summer, after a gestation period of seven months. The young weigh from five to seven pounds at birth but within eight or nine days they have nearly doubled their weight and can easily outrun a man. The young are weaned at about five months of age. Only females care for the fawns.

Except during the fall mating season (called rut), males

and females tend not to associate. Bucks are found primarily in male-only groups, while does occur with their fawns or yearling females. Does become more communal in autumn and several does and their fawns may forage together. The does in these groups are often related whereas no such kinship bonds are apparent in male groups.

In the North American desert region, deer can be migratory, using habitats at higher elevations in summer and moving down-slope in winter to escape cold temperatures and find better food resources. Distances covered during these migrations range from a few to over 100 miles and are made by individuals or small bands.

Other than man, adult deer have few predators. Mountain Lions are the only regular predators of deer, some cats killing fifty or more per year. Wolves have been eliminated in all desert regions leaving the smaller Coyote as the only canine predator. Coyote predation can be an important cause of death for fawns and in some regions may be responsible for up to 40% of fawn mortality. An eyewitness account by Kenneth Hamlin graphically reveals what can occur:

"Two Coyotes were observed 350 meters away, moving toward the deer. One Coyote came within 40 meters of the doe and fawns. When it observed the deer, the Coyote sat down and watched them. After two or three minutes, the second Coyote....circled around the deer and hid behind a juniper bush. The first Coyote then ran directly toward the doe and fawns. When it saw the Coyote, the doe chased it about 10 meters downslope and returned to the fawns. The same Coyote immediately returned and was then chased for about 100 meters. At initiation of the second chase, the Coyote in hiding ran to the fawns and grabbed one by its head and neck. The doe rushed back and attacked the second Coyote with her forefeet (but the Coyote escaped by carrying) the fawn into a juniper bush."

Deer are primarily browsers, feeding on twigs and leaves of shrubs. However, when available, they readily consume the young green leaves of herbs and grasses.

DESCRIPTION: Deer are the only antlered mammals in the North American desert region. Mule Deer have large ears, reach 3 1/2 feet at the shoulder and attain 350 pounds in weight. White-tailed Deer are smaller, run with a bobbing gallop (mule deer bound with stiff-legged jumps), and hold their tail erect when fleeing revealing the white underside.

DISTRIBUTION: Mule Deer are uncommon throughout the North American Deserts.   White-tailed Deer are found in the northern Great Basin Desert, the eastern Sonoran Desert and the Chihuahuan Desert.   Both species remain in the vicinity of water in the summer months.

Mule Deer

Bighorn Sheep, ram - photograph by Robert L. Leatherman

You are not likely to forget a sighting of a Bighorn Sheep. Seen stationed on some precipitous cliff, the muscular torso and massive horns of a 185-pound ram is a scene befitting any postcard or travel brochure. It's also a scene usually reserved for the more adventurous hiker who climbs up into the desert ranges in search of this timid species.

Bighorn Sheep, Ovis canadensis, generally vacate regions of human activity, preferring an isolated existence far removed from mankind. Open terrain with broad vistas and steep, boulder-strewn slopes are their preferred habitat. In such areas they are found from hillsides of only a few hundred feet to over 10,000 feet in some of the highest desert mountains. Brush-covered slopes are usually left to other hoofed mammals such as deer or burros.

The ancestors of Bighorn Sheep evolved in Eurasia during the early Pleistocene epoch, beginning some 2.5 million years ago. By the late Pleistocene, they had migrated across the Bering Land Bridge into North America, eventually spreading far south into Mexico. The Bighorn has persisted to this day by occupying steep rugged terrain and existing on plant material other herbivores could not utilize.

Although today their range and numbers are shrinking due to habitat destruction, competition with feral livestock, and the introduction of exotic diseases, as a group the genus Ovis has been remarkably successful. Close relatives of Bighorn Sheep exist in Europe and Asia as well as North America; a distribution unmatched by few other mammalian groups. They are still common in both Canada and Eurasia though many other Pleistocene or "Ice-age" mammals have since become extinct.

The Bighorn Sheep's ability to traverse rocky terrain is legendary. Perhaps only the Mountain Goat is more sure-footed. I have seen adult rams run and leap about canyon walls that would defy any mountain climber. Their power derives from a heavy musculature, observable from even a moderate distance. In addition, sheep hooves flatten out like tough sponges on rocks, maximizing friction and thus reducing slippage. (Yet even with these adaptations, the dangerous nature of their home terrain is such that sheep have been known to die as a result of cliff falls.) Sheep are confident of their climbing skills and use them as their chief means of escape from predators.

A second feature giving Bighorn an edge over other herbivores is a digestive system which enables them to utilize food other animals avoid. Sheep must often browse on dry, hard, abrasive plant material of poor quality. To maximize the removal of nutrients, each food mass is subjected to a complex of digestive processes. First, the food is chewed using the sheep's broad molars--teeth which in young animals regenerate themselves to compensate for wear. Next the food mass is transported to the rumen. There it is partly digested by bacteria which are critical in converting plant cellulose to energy. From the rumen it is moved into the reticulum where it is predigested and regurgitated back into the mouth for rumination. While ruminating, or "chewing the cud," the food is mixed with saliva and thoroughly chewed, then reswallowed into the omasum where further digestion occurs. Finally the food passes into the true stomach. From the stomach, the food passes into the small intestine where more nutrients are absorbed. It is then dumped into the caecum, another fermentation vat, where bacteria convert what is left into additional nutrients. The remainder passes out of the caecum and into the large intestine where it is concentrated into the pellet droppings often found on hillside trails.

Other than man, sheep have few enemies that regularly prey upon them. I have learned of just two attacks by Golden Eagles. One in which a lamb was captured and a second in which an apparently healthy ram was killed by two adult eagles. Mountain Lions are known to occasionally prey upon sheep although the impact of this predator on desert sheep populations appears to be minor. There are many accounts of Coyotes pursuing Bighorn and they sometimes capture unprotected lambs or injured adults, but healthy adult sheep usually have no difficulty dealing with these small canines.

Bighorn do not require drinking water in winter when green vegetation is available. However, during the summer months they visit waterholes at least every three days. They can tolerate up to a 20% decrease in body weight as a result of water loss and often look emaciated when coming in to drink. However, within minutes they have replenished the lost water and appear trim and strong. The capacity to drink quickly and rehydrate within minutes is no doubt an adaptation to increased predation around waterholes.

DESCRIPTION: The spectacular curled horns of the males or "rams" immediately identify Bighorn Sheep. Females or "ewes" have much narrower horns that rarely exceed fifteen inches in curl. Both sexes are tan to brown in color. Adult males weigh 140 to 220 pounds; females 75 to 130 pounds. Sheep from desert ranges are considerably smaller than those from the Rocky Mountains.

DISTRIBUTION: Can be expected throughout many of the desert ranges in the Southwest but numbers are small and distribution is spotty. In general, sheep in desert ranges are declining in number and have become extinct in eighteen desert ranges where they occurred within historical times. Prefers rocky canyons and hillsides though is occasionally seen on the flats in winter moving from one desert range to another.

A Final Comment

A few years ago, my goal of enlightening the public a-bout our desert wildlife might have ended at this point. But today additional comments are necessary for there is doubt about how many of the species described in this book will still exist when my children are grown. I would like to think that they would have the same opportunities that I had: to watch a Bighorn Sheep bound up a precipitous cliff, a Kit Fox bring a kangaroo rat to its young, or a Desert Tortoise construct its burrow. It only seems right that our heirs would not be denied these privileges.

My concern involves both the numbers and behavior of the human species. Five decades ago one vehicle, a single marksman or a lone prospector put little strain upon the des-ert environment since the desert's awesome expanse guaran-teed its recovery. However today the number of humans vi-siting, working and living in our deserts has reached into the millions and the damage is outstripping the recovery powers of this very delicate land.

A massive education program is needed. A program that explains the fragile nature of the desert environment; a pro-gram that changes our behavior by making us more sensitive about the impacts of our actions and the demands upon the desert environment by an ever-expanding human population.

Rocky wash habitat, Carlsbad Caverns National Park

Selected Bibliography

The books listed below represent some of the references used in the preparation of this volume. Each is written in a style suitable for lay users and should be consulted for more detailed information.

Brown, G. W., Jr. 1968 (volume 1) and 1974 (volume II). Desert Biology. Academic Press, New York, New York.

Cloudsley-Thompson, J. L. 1968. Spiders Scorprions Centipedes and Mites. Pergamon Press, Oxford, England.

Leydet, Francois. 1977. The Coyote: Defiant Songdog of the West. Chronicle Books, San Francisco, California.

Louw, Gideon and Mary Seely. 1982. Ecology of Desert Organisms. Longman, Inc., New York, New York.

Miller, Alden H. and Robert C. Stebbins. 1964. The Lives of Desert Animals in Joshua Tree National Monument. University of California Press, Berkeley, California.

Monson, Gale and Lowell Sumner. 1980. Desert Bighorn. The University of Arizona Press, Tucson, Arizona.

National Geographic Society. 1983. Field Guide to the Birds of North America. The National Geographic Society, Washington D. C.

Ryan, R. M. 1968. Mammals of Deep Canyon. Palm Springs Desert Museum, Palm Springs, California.

Schmidt-Nielsen, Knut. 1964. Desert Animals: Physiological Problems of Heat and Water. Oxford University Press, Oxford, England.

Smith, Robert L. 1982. Venomous Animals of Arizona. College of Agriculture, The University of Arizona, Tucson.

Sowls, Lyle K. 1984. The Peccaries. The University of Arizona Press, Tucson, Arizona.

Stebbins, Robert C. 1985. A Field Guide to Western Reptiles and Amphibians. Houghton Mifflin Company, Boston.

Wauer, Roland H. 1985. A Field Guide to Birds of the Big Bend. Texas Monthly Press, Inc., Austin, Texas.

Weathers, Wesley W. 1983. Birds of Southern California's Deep Canyon. University of California Press, Berkeley.

State and National Park Animal Checklist

SELECTED VERTEBRATE ANIMALS IN STATE AND NATIONAL PARKS

	Anza-Borrego Desert St. Park, CA	Arches Nat. Park, UT	Big Bend Nat. Park, TX	Canyon de Chelly Nat. Mon., AZ	Carlsbad Caverns Nat. Park, NM	Casa Grande Nat. Mon., AZ	Death Valley Nat. Mon., CA	Grand Canyon Nat. Park, AZ	Joshua Tree Nat. Mon., CA	Lake Mead National Rec. Area, NV	Lehman Caves Nat. Mon., NV	Mitchell Caverns St. Reserve, CA	Organ Pipe Cactus Nat. Mon., AZ	Petrified Forest Nat. Park, AZ	Saguaro Nat. Mon., AZ	Tonto Nat. Mon., AZ	Valley of Fire St. Park, NV	White Sands Nat. Mon., NM	Wupatki Nat. Mon., AZ	Zion Nat. Park, UT
Couch's Spadefoot Toad	-	-	x	-	x	x	-	-	-	-	-	x	x	x	x	-	-	x	-	-
Red-Spotted Toad	x	x	x	x	x	-	x	x	x	x	x	x	x	x	x	x	x	x	-	x
Desert Tortoise	x	-	-	-	-	x	x	-	x	x	-	x	x	-	x	x	x	-	-	-
Texas Banded Gecko	-	-	x	-	x	-	-	-	-	-	-	-	-	-	-	-	-	-	-	-
Banded Gecko	x	-	-	-	-	x	x	x	x	-	-	x	x	-	x	x	x	-	-	x
Zebra-tailed Lizard	x	-	-	-	x	x	x	x	x	x	x	x	x	-	x	-	x	-	-	-
Greater Earless Lizard	-	-	x	-	x	-	-	-	-	-	-	-	-	-	x	x	-	x	-	-
Lesser Earless Lizard	-	-	-	x	-	-	-	-	-	-	-	-	-	x	x	-	-	x	x	-
Desert Iguana	x	-	-	-	-	x	x	x	x	-	x	x	-	x	-	x	-	-	-
Short-Horned Lizard	-	x	-	x	-	-	-	-	-	-	-	-	-	x	x	x	-	x	x
Desert Horned Lizard	x	-	-	-	-	x	x	x	x	x	x	x	-	-	x	-	-	x
Regal Horned Lizard	-	-	-	-	x	-	-	x	-	-	-	x	-	x	x	-	-	x
Round-tailed Horned Lizard	-	-	x	-	x	-	-	-	-	-	-	-	-	-	-	-	x	-	-
Chuckwalla	x	-	-	-	-	x	x	x	x	-	x	x	-	x	x	-	-	x
Desert Spiny Lizard	x	x	x	x	x	x	x	x	x	x	x	x	-	x	x	x	x	x
Eastern Fence Lizard	-	x	x	x	x	-	-	x	-	x	-	-	x	x	-	-	x	x	x
Side-Blotched Lizard	x	x	x	x	x	x	x	x	x	x	x	x	x	x	x	x	x	x	x	x
Gila Monster	-	-	-	-	x	-	x	-	x	-	-	x	-	x	x	?	-	-	-
Plateau Whiptail	-	x	-	x	-	-	-	-	-	-	-	x	-	-	-	x	x
Western Whiptail	x	x	x	-	x	x	x	x	x	x	-	x	x	x	x	x	x
Common Kingsnake	x	-	x	-	x	x	x	x	x	x	x	x	-	x	x	x	x	-	x
Desert Striped Whipsnake	-	x	x	x	-	x	x	1	x	x	x	2	x	-	2	?	-	x	x
Coachwhip	x	x	x	-	x	x	x	x	x	x	-	x	x	x	x	x	x	-	x
Gopher Snake	x	x	x	x	x	x	x	x	x	x	x	x	x	x	x	x	x	x	x	x
Western Coral Snake	-	-	-	-	x	-	-	-	-	-	-	x	-	x	x	-	-	-
Sidewinder	x	-	-	-	x	x	-	x	x	-	x	x	-	x	-	x	-	-
Western Rattlesnake	x	x	?	x	x	-	-	x	x	-	x	-	-	x	x	x	-	x	x	x
Western Diamondback	x	-	x	-	x	-	-	-	x	x	-	x	-	x	-	x	-	-
Mojave Rattlesnake	-	-	x	-	x	x	x	x	x	-	x	x	-	x	x	-	x	-	-
Turkey Vulture	x	x	x	x	x	x	x	x	x	x	x	x	x	x	x	x	x	x	x	x
Black Vulture	-	-	x	-	-	-	-	-	-	-	-	-	x	-	-	-	-	-
Red-Tailed Hawk	x	x	x	x	x	x	x	x	x	x	x	x	x	x	x	x	x	x	x
Prairie Falcon	x	x	x	x	-	x	x	x	x	x	x	x	x	x	x	x	x	x	x
Gambel's Quail	x	-	x	-	-	x	x	x	x	3	x	x	-	x	x	x	x	-	x
Scaled Quail	-	-	x	-	x	-	-	-	-	-	-	-	-	x	-	-	x	-
Mourning Dove	x	x	x	x	x	x	x	x	x	x	x	x	x	x	x	x	x	x	x	x
White-Winged Dove	x	-	x	-	x	x	-	-	x	x	-	x	x	-	x	x	?	-	-	-
Roadrunner	x	-	x	-	x	x	x	x	x	-	-	x	x	x	x	x	x	x	x	x
Barn Owl	x	-	x	-	x	x	-	-	x	x	-	x	x	-	-	?	x	x	-	x
Screech Owl	x	x	x	-	x	-	x	x	x	x	-	x	x	-	x	x	x	x	-	x
Great Horned Owl	x	x	x	x	x	x	x	x	x	x	x	x	x	x	x	x	x	x	x	x
Burrowing Owl	x	x	x	x	-	x	-	x	x	x	x	x	x	x	?	x	x	x	-
Elf Owl	-	-	x	-	-	-	-	-	-	-	-	x	-	x	x	-	-	-
Costa's Hummingbird	x	-	-	-	x	x	x	x	x	-	-	x	-	x	x	-	-	-	-
Black-chinned Hummingbird	x	x	x	x	x	x	-	x	x	x	x	x	-	x	x	x	x	x	x
Common Raven	x	x	x	x	x	x	x	x	x	x	x	x	x	x	x	x	x	x	x	x
Chihuahuan Raven	-	-	x	-	x	-	-	-	-	-	-	-	-	-	-	-	-	-	-

	Anza-Borrego Desert St. Park, CA	Arches Nat. Park, UT	Big Bend Nat. Park, TX	Canyon de Chelly Nat. Mon., AZ	Carlsbad Caverns Nat. Park, NM	Casa Grande Nat. Mon., AZ	Death Valley Nat. Mon., CA	Grand Canyon Nat. Park, AZ	Joshua Tree Nat. Mon., CA	Lake Mead National Rec. Area, NV	Lehman Caves Nat. Mon., NV	Mitchell Caverns St. Reserve, CA	Organ Pipe Cactus Nat. Mon., AZ	Petrified Forest Nat. Park, AZ	Saguaro Nat. Mon., AZ	Tonto Nat. Mon., AZ	Valley of Fire St. Park, NV	White Sands Nat. Mon., NM	Wupatki Nat. Mon., AZ	Zion Nat. Park, UT
Cactus Wren	x	-	x	-	x	x	-	-	x	x	-	x	x	-	x	x	x	x	-	-
Sage Thrasher	x	x	x	x	x	x	x	x	x	x	x	x	x	x	x	x	x	-	x	x
Bendire's Thrasher	-	x	-	-	-	x	x	-	?	-	-	x	x	x	x	-	-	-	-	x
Curve-billed Thrasher	-	-	x	-	x	x	-	-	-	-	-	-	x	x	x	?	-	x	-	-
Le Conte's Thrasher	x	-	-	-	-	x	-	-	x	x	-	x	x	-	-	-	x	-	-	x
Crissal Thrasher	x	-	x	-	x	x	-	-	x	-	x	x	-	x	x	x	?	x	-	-
Phainopepla	x	-	x	-	x	x	x	x	x	-	x	x	-	x	x	x	x	-	-	x
Loggerhead Shrike	x	x	x	x	x	x	x	x	x	x	x	x	x	x	x	x	x	x	x	x
Black-Throated Sparrow	x	x	x	x	x	x	x	x	x	x	x	x	x	x	x	x	x	x	x	x
House Finch	x	x	x	x	x	x	x	x	x	x	x	x	x	x	x	x	x	x	x	x
Western Pipistrel	x	x	x	x	x	x	x	x	x	x	x	x	x	x	x	x	x	x	x	x
Brazilian Freetail Bat	x	x	x	x	x	x	x	x	x	x	x	x	x	x	x	x	x	x	x	x
Leafnose Bat	x	-	-	-	-	x	x	?	x	x	-	x	x	-	x	x	x	-	-	-
Spotted Skunk	x	x	x	x	x	-	x	x	x	x	x	x	-	x	x	x	x	-	x	x
Striped Skunk	x	x	x	x	x	-	x	x	?	x	x	-	x	x	x	x	?	x	x	x
Hooded Skunk	-	-	x	-	-	-	-	-	-	-	-	-	x	-	x	-	-	-	-	-
Hognose Skunk	-	-	x	-	x	-	-	-	-	-	-	-	x	-	x	x	-	x	-	-
Coyote	x	x	x	x	x	x	x	x	x	x	x	x	x	x	x	x	x	x	x	x
Kit Fox	x	-	x	x	x	-	x	-	x	x	-	x	x	x	x	-	x	-	x	x
Gray Fox	x	x	x	x	x	-	x	x	x	x	x	x	x	x	x	x	x	x	x	x
Bobcat	x	x	x	x	x	-	x	x	x	x	x	x	x	x	x	x	x	x	x	x
Rock Squirrel	-	x	x	x	x	-	?	x	-	x	x	x	x	x	x	x	x	-	x	x
Roundtail Ground Squirrel	x	-	-	-	-	x	x	-	x	x	-	x	x	-	x	-	?	-	-	-
Texas Antelope Squirrel	-	-	x	-	x	-	-	-	-	-	-	-	-	-	-	-	-	-	-	-
Yuma Antelope Squirrel	-	-	-	-	-	-	-	?	-	-	-	x	-	x	x	-	-	-	-	-
Whitetail Antelope Squirrel	x	x	-	x	-	-	x	?	x	x	x	x	-	x	-	-	x	-	x	x
Ord's Kangaroo Rat	-	x	x	x	x	x	-	x	-	x	x	-	x	x	x	-	x	x	x	x
Merriam Kangaroo Rat	x	-	x	-	x	x	-	x	-	x	x	-	x	x	x	-	x	x	x	-
Silky Pocket Mouse	-	-	-	x	x	-	x	-	x	-	-	-	-	x	x	-	x	x	x	-
Little Pocket Mouse	x	-	-	-	-	x	x	-	x	x	x	x	-	-	-	x	-	x	-	-
Desert Pocket Mouse	x	-	x	-	x	x	?	-	?	x	-	-	x	-	x	-	x	-	-	-
Deer Mouse	x	x	x	x	x	-	x	x	x	x	x	x	-	x	x	x	x	x	x	x
Cactus Mouse	x	-	x	-	x	x	x	x	x	x	-	x	x	-	x	x	x	x	-	x
Brush Mouse	x	x	x	x	x	-	x	x	x	x	-	?	-	x	x	-	x	-	x	x
Desert Woodrat	x	x	-	-	-	x	x	x	x	x	x	x	x	-	x	-	x	-	-	-
Whitethroat Woodrat	x	-	x	x	x	x	-	x	-	x	-	x	x	x	x	-	x	x	x	-
Nuttall Cottontail	-	-	-	-	-	-	?	x	-	x	x	-	-	-	-	-	x	-	-	x
Desert Cottontail	x	x	x	x	x	x	x	x	x	x	-	x	x	x	x	x	x	x	x	x
Antelope Jackrabbit	-	-	-	-	-	-	-	-	-	-	-	-	-	x	-	x	-	-	-	-
Blacktail Jackrabbit	x	x	x	x	x	x	x	x	x	x	x	x	x	x	x	x	x	x	x	x
Peccary	-	-	x	-	-	-	-	-	-	-	-	-	x	-	x	x	-	-	-	-
Wild Burro	-	-	-	-	-	-	x	x	x	x	-	x	-	-	-	-	?	-	-	-
Whitetail Deer	-	-	x	-	-	-	-	-	-	-	-	-	x	-	x	-	-	-	-	-
Mule Deer	x	x	x	x	x	-	x	x	x	x	x	x	x	x	x	x	x	x	x	x
Bighorn Sheep	x	-	x	-	-	-	x	x	x	x	-	?	x	-	-	-	?	-	-	x

(1 = Striped Racer, _Masticophis_ _lateralis_; 2 = Sonoran Whipsnake, _M._ _bilineatus_; 3 = California Quail)

James W. Cornett is Curator of Natural Science at the Palm Springs Desert Museum. He holds both B.A. and M.S. degrees in biology and is the author of numerous publications on desert plants and animals. He has traveled extensively through all of the North American deserts and has lived within two, the Mojave and Sonoran, for the past seventeen years.